D1553224

MAXIMUM SECURITY

MAXIMUM SECURITY

LETTERS FROM CALIFORNIA'S PRISONS

EDITED BY EVE PELL AND MEMBERS

OF THE PRISON LAW PROJECT

INTRODUCTION BY FAY STENDER

E. P. DUTTON & CO., INC. | NEW YORK | 1972

Acknowledgments

Appreciation and thanks
to Loretta Carter, who typed the letters from longhand; to the lawyers and
legal workers who brought in special letters; to the Department of Corrections for a one-year period when convicts were allowed to send sealed letters
to attorneys; to Gregory Armstrong, editor, who cared and worked hard;
to Neal and Oriane Stender, whose mother was often away.

Published simultaneously in Canada by
Clarke, Irwin & Company Limited, Toronto and Vancouver

Library of Congress Catalog Card Number: 77-165596
SBN 0-525-15428-0

This book is dedicated to all prisoners in the Adjustment Centers of California and to three outsiders who have cared:

Edwin T. Caldwell
Frank L. Rundle
James F. Smith

To those of you who doubt that any or all of these events are true, I can only say sleep, innocent child, sleep. To awake is to become mad.

Roosevelt Williams
Soledad Prison, 1971

We convicts have begun to do our bit—writing, drawing, talking —coming out from under *our* way, in whatever way we can. I want to remember all this myself, and I have remembered some of it already. I have remembered it in all my writings, which are considerable (four years' worth), and although that hasn't amounted to very much yet, it doesn't mean that it won't come to something. In everything I do—I remember this, sitting, standing, eating, WAITING, and even sleeping—I remember it with my feet, my eyes, my hands, nerves—all.

And I believe this is good, for a man is part of what he remembers. He is also part of what he forgets, but to hell with that. If the human race is going to start coming out from under, it must come out in whatever way it can, from the lowest to the highest, and I just want the world to know it—the convict race is coming out, too. It is already out, if not in everybody, me—I am coming out for my brother convict.

James Ralph Williamson

Introduction by Fay Stender*

The horror of prison isn't even absorbable. Words don't even begin to get at it. Working with the prisoners as I do is like being present at Dachau.

A prison psychiatrist I know comes out of prison each day with his neck swollen. I felt very close to him when he told me about it. It is just the same way with me. My whole throat just tightens up. He was struggling with the dilemma of being involved in the prisons in any way at all. He was newer to it than I was. And I think he was just getting drowned in the experience of helpless rage. He's torn between staying and doing the little bit he can do, or leaving altogether. By staying, he can increase the medication a little, the tranquilizers and the pills and ease the prisoners' pain. But he cannot treat the source of the prisoners' problems. Even if he had the time, the prison wouldn't allow it, because it is part of the problem itself. At times, I have the same sense of impotence. As a lawyer, I can only offer the prisoners so much help. I have to work through a legal system which is almost completely stacked against them. In the prisons, convicts are literally at the mercy of an arbitrary system which is almost completely above and beyond the law. I have to be very careful not to hold out any false hope to the prisoners. Prisoners have little or no recourse whatsoever to the courts of law for most of the charges which are brought against them for offenses they are accused of committing in prison. An accusation, and the word of

* Adapted from an interview with Eve Pell and Gregory Armstrong.

the guard is usually sufficient to convict. As C. J. Fitzharris, the former superintendent of Soledad remarked, "If the guard takes the trouble to write something up, there must be something to it." During disciplinary hearings in the prison, an inmate has no right to counsel and no right to call any witnesses in his own behalf. Since the results of these hearings become a permanent part of his record, conviction can literally end any chance he has for parole.

For me, the prisons represent a form of pure evil. It is present no matter where you cut into them. Even when the prison authorities are on their best behavior with visitors, they exude a kind of gratuitous malignity. Once there was a black inmate who asked me if I would send him his Christmas package. Each inmate gets just one Christmas package. They give the inmate a special printed form. He writes his own name and his number on it in his own handwriting. The sender is supposed to paste that on the Christmas package so there is no possibility of any mistake when it comes to the prison. So I packaged it and sent it two weeks early. On Christmas Eve I got it back at my office in Berkeley. It said on the package: "Not on approved correspondence list." They had sent it back. They hadn't given it to him, even though they knew it was a Christmas package, his one and only package. It was Christmas Eve and still they had sent it back. On New Year's Day I went down and I took the package with me. And a very interesting thing happened. I went into "O" wing and two people whom I had never met before, program administrators, came up to me and said almost the same thing. "Hello, Mrs. Stender, I'm so-and-so. I'm not such a bad guy." And I said, "Well, if you are not such a bad guy, maybe you'll help me with Madison Flower's Christmas package. . . ." And I told them the story. The first one said he didn't have time and couldn't be bothered with it. The second one was so embarrassed that he went to the office and made the necessary arrangements. And now comes the strange thing. The package was very large, and I had dropped it, but I didn't hear anything break. But I will concede that it is possible that the instant coffee broke at that time. But when Madison Flowers got it, they had sprinkled the open glass throughout the cookies and into the cigarettes. They opened everything and they sort of made it a big mishmash of glass, instant coffee, cookies.

Once I was interviewing an inmate in chains (all the prisoners in Soledad's "O" wing are shackled and chained when they leave their cells for visits). A public-relations man for the prison brought in coffee for me, but none for the prisoner. I asked him, "Aren't you going to bring any coffee for Mr. So-and-so?" And he replied, "Oh, he can't drink it with chains." But when he saw the look on my face, he brought the coffee.

When I first went to see George Jackson at Soledad, the prison authorities brought him down in chains. They intended to have a guard with us in the room. I was able to get them to take the man out of the room, but they wouldn't take off the chains. So I went to see Captain Moody, who also refused to remove them. Finally, I went to the superintendent of the prison, Fitzharris. I told him that I had come to see George Jackson as a lawyer. I didn't know whether I would take his case or not, but I was not afraid of him. I told him that I had never seen anybody in chains before and it disturbed me. I informed him that if he would remove them, I would sign a waiver releasing him from any responsibility. He said he wouldn't because the man was dangerous, highly dangerous. I asked him if George had been charged with anything within the institution, if he had been charged with murder within the institution. And he said no. So I said, "Well, then he's innocent until proven guilty. He's done nothing, he's done nothing whatsoever. All he has is a charge, and he is presumed innocent. So take off the chains." Still he refused. So I said, "Well, look, there is nothing more I can do. I'll go back and see him. But you leave me absolutely no choice. I'll have to go to a Federal court and I don't mean that as a threat, but you know I'll have to do that because you don't give me any choice." And so he said, "Well, I take it as a threat, but of course you can do what you want." He added, "Of course, now he's missed his lunch." I can't remember if he rubbed his hands together when he said those words, but I think he did. And I just looked at him. And he realized that he had made a mistake. And he said, "Oh no, that's all right, he can have lunch. Yes, he can have his lunch."

Working in the prison has deepened my cynicism about liberalism. I am convinced that the prison is a totally lawless agency. Prison administrations attempt to conceal this. They have public-relations people whose job it is to tell lies to the public. I haven't figured out yet how many of them actually believe their own lies and how many believe that they actually have to do the things they do. I mean they'll tell you, "We don't put a man in a strip cell, he puts himself there. If he hadn't torn up his toilet or gone on that hunger strike or done that thing or caused that agitation, he would never have been put into a strip call." They really think it's possible for people to live under the conditions in which they are made to live and not react.

The prison authorities have said that I'm too involved with the inmates. It is true that I think more about the inmates' feelings than about what they have done. The prison authorities are all hung up on events that have taken place as many as ten years ago, or more. They try to provoke the prisoners so they can justify treating them so badly. If you can provoke them into doing something, then they can say, "You see."

Once I was coming out of "O" wing still reeling under the impact of the experience. I had been walking along the tier, shaking hands with the men through the slots between the bars. The minority consultant to Procunier, the head of the California Board of Corrections came up to me and said, "Oh, Mrs. Stender, we're so afraid when you put your hands in the cells that they are going to take a razor and cut your hand off." That sums up their view of these men.

Since I have begun to identify with the prisoners, it has changed my life. That is the real secret of why all these people write to me. They know that I really identify with them and care for them, sort of like my family. I can't think that I love every single one of them, but I love a whole lot of them. And it is a one-to-one, an equal emotional relationship. The only way it is unequal is that I'm out and they're in. But they know I can't do anything about that and that if I could, I would.

Once I know a particular person inside, I feel personally involved with their being locked up. I feel as badly about that person being in as I would about somebody in my family.

I certainly feel that, person for person, prisoners are better human beings than you would find in any random group of people. They are more loving. They have more concern for each other. They have more creative human potential. It is true that they often lose touch with reality. They are not realistic about what is politically possible. It is very hard to convince them that they can get any sympathy or respect whatever from the system or the law. And, in a way, it is very important for them not to allow themselves to be convinced. Prisoners who actually think that they can get justice from the system are usually the ones who go mad. They become unreal people, broken, deceived, deluded.

From the outside, the courts look superficially reasonable, but once you see what is inside, you understand that America and its economic system rests on locking people up. It is based on a few people having a lot, and a lot of people in the middle having something, and finally those people with nothing at all who are being brutalized in "O" wing.

The courts of law in this country dress up this ugly reality in fancy clothes. They drape the flag around and talk about justice and go through all kinds of mumbo jumbo to make everyone feel that it is a sacred ritual. It is this dress-up law that hides the reality of prison, and makes humane people put up with the reality of "O" wing.

With all that I have learned about justice and prisoners in this country, I don't even like standing up in the court anymore to pay my respects. You can't stand in a court where people are in chains and feel that you have anything to do with that. The only possible justification for being there is in fighting for the defendant. You can't even conceive of any identification with what the institution is doing.

Someday I'll stand up and I'll say, "I want the record to show that I'm standing up so I can stay here, and it is not meant to show any respect whatsoever."

Note

The letters in this book were written to lawyers during a period when the California Department of Corrections permitted prisoners to write sealed, uncensored letters to attorneys. (That permission has since been rescinded.) Most of the letters are addressed to Fay Stender, a Berkeley lawyer who became involved with the prison system through her participation in the legal defense of George Jackson, one of three black prisoners accused of murdering a guard while incarcerated at Soledad. She became familiar with prison conditions because she spent several months interviewing more than a hundred inmates who were potential witnesses in George Jackson's case. Many of those inmates had been moved from Soledad to other prisons throughout California. Patti Roberts and Elaine Wender are young lawyers assisting in that case; several letters are addressed to them and some to David Sklare of the San Francisco National Lawyers Guild Prison Committee.

These lawyers entered prisons and spoke with inmates. Word spread throughout the system that they were concerned with prison conditions; they were soon deluged with letters.

The California Prison System

Men and women convicted of felonies (serious crimes) are sent to prison. Prison is not the same as jail: a person convicted of a misdemeanor or being held for pretrial detention stays in jail. Although frequently people remain in jail for many months, jails are supposed to be for short-term stays. County or city governments administer jails.

The California Department of Corrections headquartered in Sacramento administers a statewide system of prisons. A man* convicted of a felony enters the system through one of two reception and guidance centers: the California Medical Facility at Vacaville or the California Institution for Men at Chino, where doctors, counselors, and other staff members examine, test, and observe him for six weeks. They take his history and record it in a central file which will follow him throughout his stay in prison. The convict's age, prior record, test results, and likelihood of violence or escape determine the institution to which he is sent.

In the letters, prisoners refer to the twelve institutions for male felons in California; each is geared to a particular type of offender. Conservation centers at Susanville, Jamestown, and Chino train prisoners who are considered low escape risks for work in one of approximately thirty conservation camps scattered throughout the state. Deuel Vocational Institution at Tracy is especially for young inmates too difficult for juvenile facilities: California Medical Facility is for inmates with psychiatric disorders; Cali-

* There are no letters from women prisoners in the book.

fornia Men's Colony West is for old men. The California Correctional Institution at Tehachapi, California Institution for Men at Chino, North Facility at Soledad, and California Men's Colony East at San Luis Obispo are medium- and minimum-security prisons. San Quentin and the Central Facility at Soledad are medium-close security prisons, and Folsom the maximum-security prison.

Some inmates are transferred frequently from one institution to another; others stay for many years in the same place.

Four adjustment centers—at Folsom, San Quentin, Soledad, and Palm Hall at Chino—constitute prisons within prisons. Called by inmates "the hole," these are used to punish those who break prison regulations, or for long-term confinement of those whom administrators do not want in their general population.

Perhaps one-half to one-third of all inmates at one time or another do some time in the hole—some for just a few days. However, some men spend years there, while others rotate between the general population and the hole. At any one time, there are about 700 inmates in the hole out of a total prison population of some 25,000.

The California prison system boasts of its advanced methods. One of the reforms responsible for that reputation, the indeterminate sentence, provides a minimum and a maximum term, fixed by law, for each felony. The judge presiding at trial does not fix the sentence of a convicted man; he sentences each individual to the term prescribed by law. For example, the term for armed robbery is a minimum of five years and a maximum of life; for involuntary manslaughter, from six months to fifteen years.

Indeterminate sentencing was established to make the treatment fit the criminal rather than the punishment fit the crime. The major objective of indeterminate sentencing was to release prisoners as soon as they were ready to return to society rather than hold them for an arbitrary period of years. However, statistics show that prisoners in states using indeterminate sentencing serve longer terms than prisoners serving fixed sentences.

The responsibility of determining the amount of time each prisoner must serve belongs to the Adult Authority of the Department of Corrections. This group, appointed by the governor, consists almost exclusively of retired law-enforcement officers.

Two members of the Adult Authority constitute a parole board. Parole boards travel from prison to prison, interviewing and deciding whether or not to parole prisoners.

In order to be eligible for parole, a man must have served a given percentage of his minimum sentence; his record must indicate that he is ready to return to society. In order to present a good record to the board, prisoners may amass work experience, further their education, join a religious group, take vocational training, and generally conform to regulations. The absence of bad reports and the prisoner's prior record weigh heavily with the board.

The parole board may set a date for the convict to leave prison or it may deny parole and make an appointment to consider him again in as short a time as a few months or as long a time as three years. Convicts serving indeterminate sentences with a maximum of life live with the fear that they may never be released. Men with recent disciplinary infractions are less likely to be paroled; men in an adjustment center are almost never paroled.

Frequently guards cite prisoners for such offenses as "magnifying grievances," "disrespect," or "agitation"; for these, the Adult Authority can deny parole for a year. Prisoners charged with serious offenses such as possession of a weapon or assault who are tried and acquitted in court often suffer penalties in prison despite their exoneration. The Adult Authority is not likely to grant them a parole date for many years.

A convict charged with breaking a prison regulation appears before a disciplinary committee of guards and prison administrators. This committee does not permit the prisoner to present evidence or examine witnesses who may appear against him; he cannot call witnesses on his behalf; he has no right to counsel. Almost invariably, the committee finds the prisoner guilty.

For punishment, prison authorities deprive the convict of one or all of the freedoms he still has: visits, the right to buy items from the prison store, exercise, yard privileges, television, and desserts. They may confine him in his own cell, or in the adjustment center in a special punishment cell, of which there are several kinds. The strip cell, a four-foot by eight-foot concrete room, may be kept dark all day or have the light on day and night. This cell may contain only a hole in the floor for plumbing and a slot in the solid steel door through which a special "restricted diet" is pushed twice a day: a ball of leftovers pressed together and baked, served with a slice of bread and a limited amount of water. Sometimes the prisoner is kept naked, with only a blanket for bedding on the concrete floor. The prisoner is isolated for days or weeks at a time from other human beings.

This extreme punishment is applied to men who, in one form or another, do not conform to prison standards. Many men feel they are victims of an unjust society, and once convicted begin to develop a consciousness which leads them to turn their energies into social protest. They may try to organize prisoners, often along ethnic lines; they challenge the legitimacy of the system that holds them.

The letters in this book were written by convicted felons; most of those whose writing is represented here have spent long periods of time confined in adjustment centers throughout the state. For that reason, the letters as a whole do not represent the experience of the average inmate who adjusts to the system, does his time, and gets out. Many of the writers are black or chicano; few have known a stable or middle-class life, or had much formal education. State authorities placed many of them in foster homes when they were children, then placed them in juvenile halls, Youth Authority institutions and, finally, prison. These men represent a pattern as clearly defined as the more familiar middle-class progress from high school to college to graduate school or career.

The letters as printed have been selected from thousands. They have been cut to eliminate repetition. No changes have been made in spelling or grammar. Names of some prisoners have been changed in order to protect them.

All the men who wrote risked severe reprisals for telling the world outside what is happening to them day after day, year after year, in California prisons.

Don't be telling me what is right. You talk that right jive, but where was you when my old man and the neighbors was teaching me how to steal and shoot dope? Where was you when me and my brothers and sisters was crazy and blind from hunger? Where was you when my mama was gambling away the welfare check? Where was you when the World was calling me a dirty nigger and a greasy Mexican and a poor white peckawood? Where was you when the cops was whipping me upside my head just because my skin was dark? Where was you when I was losing respect for your law and your order? Where was you when Wrong was my only salvation? I'll tell you where you was. You was clear across town—Y'know, over there living in them big, fine houses—talking that trash about right and wrong. But check this out: There ain't no such thing as right or wrong in my world. Can you dig? Right or wrong is what a chump chooses to tell himself. And I chose to tell myself that stealing is right. I had a choice: to be a poor-ass, raggedy-ass mathafukker all my life or to go out into the streets and steal me some money so I could buy me a decent pair of shoes to wear, or shoot me some dope so I could forget about the rat-and-roach infested dump I live in. Yeah, I got a chip on my shoulder. But it didn't get up there by itself. And it's gonna stay up there until you eliminate the funky conditions that breed cats like me. Yeah, you gonna send me to the pen. But that ain't no big thing because I've been in prison all my life. And if you think you can rehabilitate me by sending me to prison, then you are sadly mistaken. How do you rehabilitate a cat who has never been "habilitated"? There ain't nothing to rehabilitate. I know why you're sending me to the pen. You're sending me there to be punished, to do some A'ems and P'ems. But, fool, don't you know that you can't get nothing down by throwing salt into my open wounds? And I want you to know one thing before I split. I ain't ashamed of what I did or who I am. I'm me—dig. I've talked that talk, and now I'm ready to walk that walk . . .

Alfred Hassan

THE PIT

Glossary of Life in "The Pit"

A.A.—The Adult Authority, a state appointed body made up for the most part of former law enforcement personnel, which functions as a parole board.

A/C—The Adjustment Center.

A 115—The number of a rule covering a wide variety of inmate offenses inside prison.

Beef—Convict term for an accusation brought by the prison authorities.

Broadway—Civilian life.

Bull—Prison guard.

Canteen—Prison store.

Date—The date set by the Adult Authority for the convict's indeterminate sentence to be ended; date of parole.

Hole—Punishment cell.

Jacket—Prisoner's record.

Joint—The prison.

Life Top—Maximum penalty of life imprisonment under California's indeterminate sentencing law, i.e. one year to life.

M.T.A.—Medical Training Assistant, inmate orderly.

R.D.—Restricted diet called a "vitamin loafe" by prison officials and a "Siberian goof ball" by inmates. It consists of a ball of leftovers (garbage) pressed together and baked. Sometimes served frozen.

R&R—Receiving and Release.

Shank—Prison-made knife.

Streets—Life outside prison.

The Pit

by Alfred Hassan

The first time I saw Folsom there were about 30 of us dressed in white muslin pajamas and handcuffs. We were staring blankly through the barred windows of the Greyhound-looking bus that had brought us from Vacaville Prison. The bus was sitting, motor still idling, in the main gate sally port like a winded deer trapped in a lion's lair, only we were the captives. I can't remember exactly how the main entrance to the prison looks because I only saw it once—and that was only for a few minutes. But I do remember the spine-chilling feeling I experienced as the prison's huge onimous walls loomed before my startled eyes like a stony gargoyle lurking behind a satanic smile.

A penetrating silence pervaded the stuffy passenger section of the bus. All of my peers, my brothers of oppression, were sitting in complete silence and staring wide-eyed at the "granite monstrosity." I felt small and very insignificant. I felt like a tiny pebble lost forever in an infinite sea of huge boulders. Suddenly, everything went into reverse. My whole life was racing away from me instead of toward me. . . .

I had just said to myself, "This sure is a cold shot," when an old brother, a four-time loser, broke the eerie silence with one of the most down-to-earth statements I had heard in a long time. The old brother, with an impish smile pasted on his wrinkled face, fixed his mouth like Humphrey Bogart and said, "Baby, this is it—this is the pit!"

To quote Caesar Ibn Moor, a brother of oppression:

". . . The physical effects of prison are produced by the state of mind and emotions. Prison is a social setting where hate and extreme paranoia constantly prevail, killing your spirit and keeping you in a state of suspicion. You carry the tension of social sickness so consistantly that it begins to feel as natural as the shirt on your back." In spite of the fact that you grow accustomed to carrying this internal turmoil, it nevertheless breeds physical and emotional illnesses and an assorted variety of other ailments which come from hypertension and general emotional conflict.

We spend the vast majority of our time vegetating and plunging deeper into the pit of Lost Souls. It is no wonder that we behave like snakes crawling around at the bottom of a deep, dark pit. When you cage a man up like an animal, how else do you expect for him to behave? No man, no matter what he has done in life, deserves to be treated like an animal. If a man has done something so bad that we can't stand to look at him, then shoot him. But don't tamper with his soul. If he is a tyrant, then relieve him of his misery with a bullet in his brain. But don't whip his mind. Don't lie to him when he knows you are lying. Don't hand him that shit about rehabilitation. Don't make promises you'll never keep. A man can stand so much. You can beat the flesh but it will soon become accustomed to the pain. But the mind is very, very tender. It can stand so much. And once the mind is gone, what do you do with the body? You put the body out on the Yard. Yeah, that's it. Walking down long corridors, in small rooms, across the neatly trimmed grass. I'm talking about the convicts who are in the Pit forever.

I swear I want to cry sometimes when I look at some of the older prisoners who have been in prison so long that they hold conversations with people who aren't there and blink their sad eyes once every four or five minutes. I swell all up inside every time I watch those old convicts shuffling aimlessly around the yard with no particular destination in mind. What they feel inside, however, is beyond my scope of knowing, and I will not

attempt to enter into their troubled minds. This would be unfair,
I think. All I can do at this stage of the game is look at my older
brothers of oppression and wonder if this will be me 15 or 20
years from now. Can I hold on? Will I last? Will I someday hold
conversations with ghosts? Will I let my mind plunge downwards
into the pit of Lost Souls, where it is cold and damp and lonely?
These are things I often think about. I try not to think about
them, but the harder I try the more vivid they become in my
mind. It is enough to make a cat shake his closed fist at the sky.
I feel this way because I know something is very wrong. It's not
right that a man should spend half of his life behind prison walls
because of a mistake he made in his youth. I know this is wrong
because I have seen what long periods of incarceration have done
to the mind—the soul. I have seen cats leave here twice as hostile,
twice as confused, twice as anti-social than they were when they
entered. Depleted of nearly all of their mental juices, they are
"thrown back" into society where they are expected to function
like normal human beings. And then society wonders why re-
cidivism is so high in the country; why a man serves five or ten
years in prison only to go out and commit the same act again.

The Pit is Hell! It is a burning, flaming hell. Cut off from society, deprived of the soft touch of a woman, relegated to the
insane world of unsavory foods, hard beds, second-hand information, needless harassment and intimidation, archaic therapeutic
programs, obsolete vocational training, inferior schools, stuffy
cells, unfair mailing and visiting privileges, racist prison guards,
violence, treachery, murder and so many other evils that you get
dizzy just thinking about them, you find yourself sometimes ques-
tioning your own existence. It's frightening. I think each night
every convict in this place thanks whatever God he believes in
for seeing him safely through the day. When I lay my head down
at night, I know I am thankful to whatever Gods exist that I
wasn't shanked to death or poisoned by the rotten food, or shot
in the head by some trigger-happy guard looking for a reputation.
But I still find myself whispering at night to somebody I can't
see. And this is a big thing coming from me because I doubt

God's existence. I am a materialist. Objectively, I know this is just a lot of nonsense. But subjectively (emotionally), I cannot help myself. Prison, I guess, has a way of playing strange tricks on the mind. It makes you so paranoid that you think everybody is scheming on you. Sometimes I get so paranoid I feel like running somewhere and hiding. But I am strong enough now to check myself. But what about tomorrow? Will there be a tomorrow? And when tomorrow gets here, will it make a difference?

Charles Silberman in his book *Crisis in Black and White* wrote in part about the oppressive conditions inside Hitler's concentration camps. He said that many of the Jews in those concentration camps patterned their personality and behavior after the Nazi prison guards. They would paint the Swastika on the sleeves of their shirts and goose-step up and down the prison yard like proud German soldiers parading before the Fuhrer. They would even inform on each other. The reason for their strange behavior was due mainly to the harsh fact that they were totally dependent on their German slavemasters for their very existence. It was a weird parent-child relationship. A small child, because it is totally dependent upon its parents, will often imitate either its mother or its father. This bizarre parent-child relationship exists here at Folsom.

The ideal prisoner is one who feels that he is absolutely dependent, one who senses (or thinks) he is inferior. His blue jean uniform gives testimony to his lowly status of degradation and inferiority. He lives in a cruel world of powerlessness. Someone else is making all the major decisions in his life. He becomes, perhaps, his own worst enemy. I imagine that it is very unkind to the soul to think yourself inferior, totally dependent on someone whose integrity you doubt. But this is the world of the prison inmate who has allowed himself to fall into the weird bag of looking at the prison officials in the same light that he viewed his parents when he was a small child. He, like the dependent child, becomes an excellent imitator. The "parent-child relation," however, becomes a two-headed monster. On the one head, the monster serves as a good little, tattle-telling child who reports all the wrongdoings of its naughty sisters and brothers to its parents. On the other head, the monster becomes an evil to the general population of the prison, for its pits prisoner against prisoner, often causing much bloodshed. The informer is the most despised and hated "thing" in any prison. But the "child-inmate" can't help himself. He's not just an ordinary child. No, no. He is the much talked about retarded child. His retardation came about as fatal consequence of his total dependency and his self-imposed feelings of inferiority, which are a result of the "dependency thing." To him, the prison guard is Big Daddy. And one must be obedient to Daddy, or one will be severely punished. It's weird.

I have seen many convicts around this place who behave just like the prison guards. They have that little air of "Guardism" about themselves. When you talk to them, you get the strange feeling that you are rapping to one of the prison guards or to one of the prison counselors. If they are in a position of leadership, say leadman on the kitchen serving line, they will often emanate an air of authority as though they had a badge pinned on their chests. For example, if you are slow on the job, they (the imitators) will drop little hints to the effect that they will make arrangements to get you fired or moved to another section of the job if you don't pick up the pace. And in many cases they have the power to do exactly what they say.

Under the California Penal System, a prisoner has no idea at all as to when he will be released to parole supervision. He can only guess. And this guessing game only infuriates him and increases his distrust of the penal system. Each time he is denied parole, his wife and children and parents are also denied. Perhaps if he knew the exact date of his release from prison, his wife and family would have something concrete to look forward to, not to mention the fact that he would be less inclined to do anything that might cause him to get his release date taken away from him. But as it stands, he does not know when he is going home. And this is very hard on his family, especially his wife if he is married.

Each time I told my wife that I had been denied parole she suffered tremendous pain. Had she known when I was coming home, I would not have had to write her all those disappointing letters. How I hated to tell her I had just been denied parole. I remember the time when I took four years to the Adult Authority (A.A.). I just knew they were going to give me a parole date. My wife wrote me a letter telling me that she sensed (woman's intuition) that I was going to get a parole date. This made me feel very good and warm inside. But the roof, the world, fell in. I was denied parole! I didn't have the heart to write my wife and tell her the sad news. I just couldn't. But the following week she came up to visit me. When I walked out on the visiting yard, she was already sitting down at the table. I knew from the way she was looking that she expected me to run up to her and hug her and tell her that I would be home in a few weeks or a few months. When I sat down at the table the first thing she asked me was when was I coming home. I swallowed hard and broke the sad news. At first she didn't believe me. She thought I was putting her on. After telling her about five or six times, I finally convinced her that I had been denied parole. When she finally accepted the truth, it seemed like all the life was draining out of her plump face. Tears came to her eyes. I had never seen her look so sad. I felt like crying myself. I knew the pain and suffering she was going through. I was hard and calloused. But my sweet Mary was so tender and soft—she couldn't understand why I had been denied parole. From that point on, my wife was a different person. I think she lost all of her soul right there on that visiting yard. A year later she got sick and died of double pneumonia. Had I been given a parole date, I truly believe that my wife would still be living today. I mean, the situation and circumstances would have been different. Even if my wife knew that I was going to be in prison for ten or twenty years, her knowing the exact date of my parole release would have given her something concrete to look forward to. There wouldn't have been all the sad letters and disappointments.

It is said that it is bad business to blame others for your mis-

givings. But I say fuck this specious reasoning. I blame the A.A.
I blame them because they are the cause of much suffering and
agony. I blame them because they are misusing and abusing their
power. I blame them because their crimes against humanity are
far greater than our petty crimes. They have the power to destroy!
And this is wrong. No such power should be in the hands of a
few men.

The Letters

Folsom
July 6, 1970

Comrade Mine:

Do you know what a world ruled by the god Perversion can be? No, on second thought, how could you? Having never seen pure horror, you could not possibly know.

Let me tell you about it.

Imagine, if you can, a world where *men* have regressed into a state of bestiality parallel to that of dogs, where they mistake other men for *women* and snarl, bite and destroy each other for their favor; where a thousand psychotics, of every conceivable description and variety, are turned loose without supervision or medical attention, spreading paranoia among the sane community members, *keepers* and *kept* alike, as liberally as the air we breath and as toxic as the deadly smog within it. A community where the products of the American Tobacco Company are a social religion, and God himself is a pack of cigarettes; where *dominos, homosexuality,* and the pursuit of cigarettes rule the mental faculties of man. A world of justice where blacks and Chicanos do more time for petty crimes and the sickness of narcotic addiction, than does a white-skin offender for rape, murder, robbery and mayhem. A business community where men are *forced* to produce products for public consumption for wages of two (2) pennies an hour; operating the most dangerous machinery without any

34

form of industrial compensation insurance; the danger of their employment is enhanced by the fact that many of them *cannot* even *read* the safety instructions on the machinery they operate! A considerate community, where visiting with one's family is *encouraged* by allowing a visitor, who has traveled more than four hundred miles, less than two (2) hours twice monthly. An urban city of steel, where two men are *forced* to live in a 4' x 9' space sixteen hours a day, and the Health and Safety Code demands that a gorilla, whether he be ten months or ten years old, have a living space of 1,065 feet! A LAW & ORDER community where administrative control is so thoroughly proficient that we've had sixteen (16) brutal community murders, countless confiscations of instruments of death, along with a boundless number of persons who have suffered A.D.W.'s. [Assaults with a Deadly Weapon] by recognized psychotics, in the mere twenty-five months that I have been forced to live in this madhouse of correction.

You are told upon arrival here that you *must adjust,* be able to *fit in,* with the scheme of this unimaginable horror *before* you will be considered *socially responsible* enough to be placed back into *free* society.

Yes, comrade mine, these and a thousand more instances represent the value of a twenty-four-hour night and daymare of society's long evolution from the cave of insensitive brutality to enlightened 20th Century.

Folsom Prison is a place where *legal* injustice nourishes a monster in the depths of man so terrible that America's favorite monster, Mr. Frankenstein, is reduced to the status of a gentle soul by comparison!

Incredible? unbelievable? Yeah, I can dig it. That's exactly what it is! But its happening, its happening every minute of every day.

> Peace AFTER the revolution,
> Thomas K. Clark

Louie E. Hall
P.O. Box A31110
Represa, Calif. 95671
May 6th, 1971

Hello Patti Roberts,

I know that you didn't take my case, but just in case you think about me one of these days when you're talking to some old run-down attorney who doesn't have but thirty or forty cases going at one time, you may think to mention me, and tell him I have in only ten years now, and that when I go back to Mississippi, I will have only another four and a half years until I will be eligible for parole, and then I can spend the rest of my life on parole, and all because a nice Southern Judge refused to let me call witnesses in my behalf, and refused to let my lawyer withdraw from my case because he said he couldn't handle it. . . .

Ah, but Patti, Patti, Patti, it sounds as if I am getting smart there, and I don't mean to be; but really, I don't understand? . . . I thought you people there were to help us who were having or have had our Civil Rights Violated . . . Christ girl! The only ones around who have had their Rights violated any more than I have had mine violated . . . are dead! I've had twenty years smashed out of me in these stinking prisons and reform schools, and Patti, I've really never been a thief, never really liked to steal or liked people that stole, and it has made me sick at times, but I was raised between two different cultures: an Indian grandmother who was born and raised on the Indian Reservation in Oklahoma, where she married an English man and then trekked to California in an old wagon at the turn of the century. I couldn't understand her world, but I was raised in the thoughts of it that she loaded onto me, and I wanted the old days, and yet I wanted the other world too, the white man's world . . . But I didn't understand any of it . . . and Patti, I got my face twisted real crooked on the inside as I was growing up, and I didn't have any idea what in the hell was going on. I am a why? man . . . But do you think I ever got any answers to any of my why?'s as was growing up?

You damn right I didn't! I would ask my half-breed and very confused mother something, and she would turn away from me and
shrug her defeated shoulders and say, "Honey, I don't know. I
don't know anything about those things . . ." And all my life, not
only did she not know, but everyone else I tried to talk to didn't
know either . . . No one knew why we were poor, no one knew
why we were afraid—and not only was it my people who were
afraid, but everyone around me seemed afraid—so I refused to be
afraid . . . If you care enough to read my criminal record, you
will see what other people think of me. I got to where I was not
afraid of the Thunder-God, or the white man's child-murdering-
God . . . But Patti, Patti, it is terribly lonely not having a god or
any friends or a love or children of my own.

Well, I've finally made the transition from the Indian world of
my grandmother, to the world of the white man, and let me tell
you, it leaves a lot to be desired!

And this man-crushing, money-making machine is slowly eating
into the life and soul and being of me. Did you know that the men
and women in prisons are nothing but cattle . . .? You didn't?
Well, let me tell you . . . These prisons are big ranches with
cattle in them, and the herders are running prisons as a business.
They get so much money to keep us herded together and dumb,
why if we really leaned something in here, we wouldn't be back,
and what of all the money they get to feed and clothe us? Hu-uh!
"Don't you talk back to me! I'm an officer," and this is said in a
very officious voice, too. "I'm going to put you to work in the
laundry."

"But, I'm a writer . . . I'm working on a novel right now."

A snicker. "I know what's good for you; I'm putting you in
the laundry. You need a trade!"

"But I have three trades now; getting a job isn't my problem."

Anyway, I went to work in the laundry. And the money just
rolls in . . . Then every few years they let us out to breed so
they will have more cattle for their slaughter-houses . . . Just
think of all those children born to convicts . . . what chance do
they have to ever find out what is happening in the world . . .?

What chance do they have of not being like their father or mother . . .? They love their mother and father, so . . . it must be all right to steal, or mom and dad wouldn't do it . . . So here is more children for the machine to suck the life and blood from, and they too will be crushed in time, and what of their children? What of their children! Oh, Christ, Patti . . . it is a vicious thing!

Can you hear me Patti, can you see me? or do the buffalo that you are trying to tame blind you to me? And, Patti, I am a very human, human being . . . I can see other people as well as myself, and I too want to help and I will. I don't have it all worked out in my mind yet, but with time, and with looking and searching, I will find a way.

I feel like I am trying to talk to you through a long tunnel, and echoing noises keep getting in the way, and even though you hold your hands cupped to your ears, and though you look around, I still can't quite believe you see or hear me . . . are you just reading the words on this paper and do you think these words are me . . .? This isn't me, this paper isn't me, these words aren't me, I'm not a folder in a law office, or a prison office; those words in my folder are only a very small part of me, something others have grabbed and put on paper—then they smiled and nodded at each other and said, "Yes, see, that's him . . . the dirty thieving bastard. Look at his record, it's all here, all the things that he's done wrong . . ." But I've done more good in this world than I have harm, I've helped more people than could be written into a hundred records. And paper can't catch a person . . . and this letter or all the letters I could write in a lifetime couldn't catch the essence that is me. I love and hate and cry and laugh and feel pain and pity and have hope and understanding in me. I have all the good things of man in me, and also all of the bad, too . . .

Well, I'm going to close; I know that you don't want to hear all this. So thanks again, and love and hope to you.

Louie (Hall)

Soledad
June 23, 1970

Dear Mrs. Fay Stender:

I came to prison in May of 1966 for Robbery. My sentence was five years to life. At that time I had a wife and three kids. Shortly after I was received in Chino Guidance Center, she and the children moved up to Oregon, her home state, for upon my release I was to be paroled to Oregon so that we may start a new life.

Even though I had been in Youth Authority and County Camp, I was considered a first termer in the eyes of the Department of Corrections, or at least that's what my legal status has me as. My first board appearance was due in November of 1967. During that 18 months before I was to see the board for consideration for a parole, I had noticed things that were highly irregular pertaining between officers and convicts. When you first come to prison, other convicts call you a "fish" until you get the hang of things. During this period of being a fish, you are always under observation not only from the prison officials, but from your fellow convicts. And during this period, depending on how you carry yourself, you're going to be labeled one of two categories—either a "regular" or "weak." The latter is what the prison authorities are constantly looking for because its these weak inmates who will be their spies and who will get up on the stand in court and tell any kind of lie that the authorities tell them to say. They do this because they are promised a variety of gifts, ranging from a transfer to a quick release date depending on how good they can be.

But it doesn't stop here, this is where it begins. If the authorities see that the "fish" isn't going to be pulled down in this filth that the prison is based upon, if he's going to be a threat to their Dictatorship that has been the way of life on the inside, then they (I am referring to the prison authorities when I say they) start the slow process of "breaking" the convict. First starts the harassment. One or more police will come into your cell while you're away and start tearing it apart. If you have personal pictures of your family, you're liable to find them either torn or in your toilet and perhaps your letters will be torn or missing. This is all done to get you to "blow it" so they have a reason then to write a 115 disciplinary report on you. But if you don't blow up, then they scheme harder. My first 115 was for having my cell mate's ducats (which is prison money) in my possession. I got off lightly, but my cell mate lost the $15 because he had asked me to go to the canteen and buy some things for him. (This was in Tracy.)

My second 115 came because I happened to be with a couple of hard-core convicts and these two people were considered a threat so the police picked us up on the yard and took us up to control. We went to a court and was asked how we plead to being drunk (sniffing glue). We plead not guilty and was found guilty on the spot. We were put in a holding cell that only has a toilet, no drinking water, and was kept there until sometime around 9:00 o'clock that night. We were packed up right after morning chow. I complained about not having nothing to eat or drink in over twelve hours and was told that I was lucky it had only been twelve hours. We finally got to the hole and did ten days for that charge. After serving the ten days I was released and told I could expect the same thing if I didn't change my ways. A few months later I was charged with taking another inmate's canteen. This inmate had not had any money during the time he was in prison so how could I have taken anything that he didn't have? I tried to explain this to the prison court, that I had witnesses who could verify my innocence, but the court ruled against me. Here was grown men playing games with my life and enjoying every minute of it. I was asked how much time did I figure I would do. My answer was around five years, this seemed to be a big joke that only they could appreciate, for I couldn't see anything funny in five years of a person's life. The result of my first encounter with the Adult Authority was a two year denial. It's no longer a secret to me why I was laughed at in the board room, because I was denied another two years last November and this time I was told I was never going to get out of prison alive.

Respectfully Yours,
Mar T. Smith

June '70
San Quentin

Dear————,

My childhood was brief. So that is how I will describe it—briefly.

By the time I was ten years old, I had lived in numerous homes, in numerous towns. Besides my mother and father (who were divorced when I was about four or five), I lived with my grandmother and grandfather, uncles and aunts, friends and neighbors. I was exposed, during those early years, to a variety of religions—each clashing with the other—and it did not take very long for me to become an atheist, which, only later, was modified to agnosticism, and even later still, to a belief, once more, in God.

I am sure, though, that the people who shared in my upbringing did the best they could with what they had. I was not treated like an orphan—well, hardly ever—and did not have to go without the necessary things of childhood, such as squirtguns and soda pop, although my people were—and still are—far from wealthy.

My mother, after my father had left, started a small antique business; like, with one old shaving mug (an heirloom) and a wagon wheel (also an heirloom). Although in the past twenty years she has built the business up somewhat, at that time it was more of an expenditure than an asset. One thing it did do, though, was absorb all her time, which made it difficult—if not impossible—raising a son. Thus, I found my home in many places, and family-life to be rather unstable.

Either I grew up fast, or not at all—which will, no doubt, be argued either way by different people. Certainly I recognized at

a tender age that a lot of people had a distorted sense of values
(an opinion I still hold to a certain degree), and would have
me accept the same. That recognition of the problem, however,
did not bring with it an understanding of the solution. I think
this is what makes a person cynical. At any rate, I was. Cynical.

My schools were like my homes: many and varied. I went to
both private, and public, schools; and, in my Junior year of high
school, quit altogether and joined the Navy to get out of town
and see the world. From then on, things moved very quickly.

I was in Naval Air, and spent a year attached to an Air Force
base in Japan; a year which, to a large extent, affected my future
—both for better and worse. I left part of me in Japan.

In December of 1963 I was discharged from the Navy, under
honorable conditions, and left immediately for Los Angeles, the
Land of Opportunity. Six months later I got married; and the
next three years brought my wife and I two children, both boys.
We also had our fair share of quarrels (Aries v. Libra), but
stuck together (as an Aries and Libra will).

Then, in January, 1967, at the age of twenty-one, I was arrested in L.A. County and charged with Murder. I had no prior
record—neither as a juvenile, nor as an adult—but had a Robbery
case pending, in which I had been released on my own recognizance. Perhaps I should digress a bit:

"O.R." bonds, generally, are not granted on Robbery cases
(at least that is what I was told by the Investigating Officer),
but there were enough extenuating factors in my favor that the
Criminal Investigator felt he could make an exception in my
case—which he did. My age; marital status; two children; a job
offer which I had received while in jail; and the fact that the
guy I was arrested with had a prior record, and was on probation
at the time: All these things entered the picture in my behalf.
Thus, I was released on my own recognizance, rather than the
$10,000 which had been set.

It was during this time, while out on bond, that I was charged
with killing my wife's "illicit lover"; she having allegedly taken
in a temporary husband while I was in jail for a month, prior to

obtaining my release. And that should bring things up to date here.

The Murder case was posted "No Bail"; so I was unable to get out of jail at any price—and spent over a year in, before I was finally convicted (of first degree), and sentenced to Life imprisonment, with seven years before eligibility for parole.

I went through the standard testing, etc, at Chino Guidance Center; and, from there, was sent here to C.T.F.-Central.

A couple of weeks after my arrival here at Soledad, a prisoner who lived a few cells down from me was raped and killed. He died of multiple stab wounds. I saw three of the four inmates involved, and also the victim as he came stumbling from his cell. In fact, I had been unknowingly talking to one of the "pointmen" while he stood watching for the officer. My only friend here at that time—a model prisoner, sixteen years older than myself —had, likewise, seen three of the four, although not the same three that I had seen. They, however, knew that we knew, which put us in a bad position, to say the least. Just our knowing who was involved, endangered our own lives; and my friend and I began holding whispered debates about the proper move for us to make, without getting our heads cut off.

One of the four was caught on the scene, but the other three —one of whom had actually raped and help stab the victim— got away. About a week later, two of them came to me and said that I was going to turn homosexual (I guess I look good), if I didn't want to end up like the man whom they had just killed, and whose blood had not even been mopped up yet. They gave me until after supper to "think it over," which was more than sufficient time, as there wasn't much to think over. I had a choice of buying some silk panties and letting my hair hang down; or getting hold of a knife, and stabbing somebody; or seeing that my keepers did their job. It was a rough decision, but I chose the latter.

I went to a Sergeant—the only official with whom I was at all acquainted—and told him that I was in danger in that wing, and wanted a move right away. He said, "Yeah, everybody wants to move," and asked for more specific details. When I ran down the situation (only my own—omitting the murder), he advised me not to "run from it." However, I remained adamant, and so a move to another wing was arranged. To this day, though, I wonder if that Sergeant actually wanted to see me get killed myself, or kill someone else. Or "turn out."

Just as a point of interest: The man who was raped and killed had anticipated it. A short while before it happened, he had been severely beaten—and raped then, too—by several inmates who were, because of it, transferred to Folsom, or somewhere. This, of course, put the victim in the position of a "snitch," even though he would not testify (so far as I know) against his assaulters, and no charges had been filed. So, when he got a visit from his people, he ran the scene down to them; about how he would be killed unless a move, or something, was arranged. His people went to the officials here and demanded protection for their son, but nothing was done. And now he's dead.

A few days after my switch (to a new wing, that is), my friend was also moved to that wing. Our debate, in regard to the murder, continued, and finally we decided to go to the Captain. An interview was set up, with an investigator from the D.A.'s office there, and we—my friend and I—explained what had really happened; what we had seen of it; and how we, ourselves, were in grave danger because of that knowledge. It was not felt, however, that there was enough evidence to obtain convictions on the three who were still running amuck. No charges were filed; and we just had to coexist with the three (one of whom has since stabbed another inmate), and their friends, as best we could.

To say that I became a nervous and paranoid wreck would be an understatement. My mother would end up crying every time she came to see me, because of my nervousness, which caused my hands to shake, and I had developed a tic in my right eye. Even some of the officials here had commented on it. One Lieutenant, who was aware of the situation, told me, "I don't know how you keep on. If I came to a prison like this, and was in your position, I would have me a murder beef in no time at all. And, if I had your amount of time to do, they would be peeling me off that fence everyday—unless I got killed."

I ate with my back to the wall. I showered with my back to the wall—and never dropped my soap, or just left it if I did. When I went to the movie, I made sure a friend was sitting behind me; and noticed everyone in the vicinity. If I went to the yard, which was seldom, I kept a gun-tower in sight. At night all my cellmate had to do was so much as move a muscle—or even think about it—and I would be wide awake. (In easier days I had always been considered a "Heavy sleeper.") And this was the way in which I had to live—if you can call it that.

An escape plot came up, in which I became involved. I had been considering it for some time, but had been hesitant on account of my case being on appeal, and hoping to see it reversed. But finally I made a move, and purchased a pipewrench, which was said to be much nicer, and quicker, than a hacksaw. For a week or two the plot thickened—until it became such a mess that I decided against it and dropped out. Now I was stuck with a pipewrench, which had cost me a lot of money; and before I could get rid of it—without junking it, of course—I got caught. This was no real big thing per se, but it dirtied my record, which, up till this time, had been kept relatively clean. It also gave me my first look at the inside of the A/C (Adjustment Center—or the Hole). I was given a 90-day program, as they call it—which was commuted after forty-five days—and returned to the mainline.

In December of that year, 1968, my mother was seriously ill; expecting to undergo surgery. Life for me here had got to the point where it was almost unbearable; and my mother's condition was the final straw. On the 30th, when the opportunity to be in on an escape presented itself, I hit the fence, along with four other men.

There had been no kind of planning, and I knew beyond all doubt that someone—if not all of us—would get shot. About the others I cannot say; but I, personally, was in a state of mind where it really didn't matter what happened. Perhaps it was a form of suicide, where I wouldn't actually have to do it myself. As it turned out, two of the inmates were shot, and no one got away. The two who had been wounded (one seriously) were taken to the hospital, and the remaining three, which included myself, placed in the Hole.

After doing twenty-nine days Isolation (a sophisticated name for Solitary Confinement), I was moved to the regular A/C section, where I would remain until after the court proceedings (on the Escape) were through.

For a short time I was acting as my own counsel, and was allowed to interview each of my witnesses. In April, I believe, one of the witnesses on my list stabbed another prisoner sixteen times (with the help of another inmate) in the neck, chest, and back, but didn't kill him (that wasn't because he didn't try, though). When I went downstairs to the Isolation section to interview him, I asked why he had stabbed the victim, with whom I was also acquainted. For reply, I got: "It's just one of those things—you know what I mean? The dude crossed me; I stuck him. That's the way it goes."

I removed that witness from my list. So he tried to kill me, also. He was—and is—a member of a clique that calls itself the "Mafia." It is comprised, almost entirely, of Mexicans; although many Mexicans consider them a disgrace to the race. In this penal system it is the most powerful clique, and credited with many, many murders and stabbings (which oftentimes amount to the same thing). It has members throughout the system—especially at Soledad, San Quentin, and Folsom—and is a menace, not only to the blacks and whites, but to other Mexicans as well. I did not know all this at that time, of course, as I had never come into contact with it—but I know now, because I have a "bounty" on my own head, payable by the Mafia.

Right about that same time, one of the five inmates on our Escape was jumped by half a dozen other prisoners—members of the Mafia. They beat and stomped him right in front of my cell (I was locked in; unable to do anything but watch it); and a month later, after he had done his Isolation time (He—and not his attackers—was charged with fighting, and sentenced to 29 days Isolation. It was easier to move one inmate than six, so the aggressors went unapprehended), the Mafia stabbed him. He lived.

Now, this prisoner was only twenty years old. He had been involved in no kind of violence whatsoever—not even a fight (his crime had been the burglarizing of the glove-compartment of a car)—and seeing him on the floor, in front of my cell, bleeding, something just made me snap inside.

I talked to the Program Administrator; told him I was sick up to here of the completely senseless violence in this prison, most of which was perpetrated by the same inmates, over and over, all because no one would testify against them. I told him that I was going to court against the prisoner who had been on my witness list (and stabbed that other guy sixteen times), if I had to escape to get there; and said that I would also be more than willing to testify against those who had jumped my crime-partner [in the escape attempt], if charges should be filed.

Few charges are filed in cases like this, though, and even fewer convictions obtained. Other prisoners won't testify: a few because of their "code"; but most because of other factors, which will be clarified somewhat as I go along.

Unless an inmate is given a parole—and many times not even then—he is not going to endanger his own life, and that of his family on the outside, by getting his name on the Mafia's shit-list, or on that of any other similar type clique—all of which are worthless, and have neither political, nor moral, tenets. The members of these cliques, many of them, have brothers on the outside who have been—and will be again—in prison themselves, and who are happy to settle a vendetta by killing someone out there. It is unfortunate that "Brotherhood" has to get a dirty name by people who believe in violence for the sake of violence.

When the D.A.'s investigator came out here to interview me on the assault case, he asked me what I expected to get for my testimony. I told him "nothing"; that I was not doing this for anything he had to offer, but for my own inner reason: the knowledge that I was doing SOMETHING, even if it killed me. He asked me if I would like a transfer after court, and I told him, "Yes, of course," though I believed his office had nothing to say in the matter of institutional transfers. He wanted to know where, and I said that Sierra Camp Center (which is a Medium-security institution) would be good; acceptable by me, anyway. As I was not eligible for minimum custody, I could not even hope (or so I believed then) for a transfer to Chino-proper (C.I.M.), or a camp. So I figured a camp center was about the next best thing, if they got me out of here soon enough.

Because of my being a prospective State's witness, I was moved from one wing to another, and placed on "Hi-power Protective Custody" (because of the danger, of course). This was a natural precaution to take, and was NOT done at my request. It was not at all necessary for me to request it, as the State takes very good care of its witnesses so far as keeping them safe—until after court, that is. I was moved into an Isolation cell on the first tier, up near the front where I would be close to the gun-rail (not because I had to do any Isolation time, but for safety.) The cell was "closed front" (that is, instead of bars on the front of the cell, where one can see out, there was only a solid door in a solid wall). Two additional locks, and a steel bar, were installed on my door to prevent bombs from being thrown into my cell through the tray slot or under the door. But, how to describe the cell . . .

When I first saw it, I just couldn't believe it. It was a dungeon. Nothing but cement and filth. I could not imagine who had lived in there before me. All day I just sat there on my bunk, in a sort of daze, staring at my new abode; and I recall saying out loud: "Remember this. Remember just what this cell looks like. Don't ever forget it."

So all day I sat there. The garbage on the floor stayed there; likewise the filth in the sink, commode, and all over the walls. I didn't see how I would ever be able to spend two days in there.

Instead of bed springs, there was a flat steel plate (which is the same throughout the Hole); the window was cemented up, except for the very top section, which was one quarter the standard size, and without any glass panes, thus exposing the occupant to all kinds of weather (the rain would actually come through, into the cell); there was no shelving whatsoever—not so much as a hook to hang a towel or clothes on (and it was against regulations to fix up a clothes line; so anyone who did so, did it at the risk of being beefed). In short, there was nothing: just four walls, and room enough to take five paces—not strides—from one end of the cell to the other. Nothing to break the monotony of cement except the usual graffiti. The window was too high for a view of anything but the roof of the wing next door. It was truly a dungeon; a tomb; a crypt. And it was "Home," for twenty-four hours a day, every day.

Maybe once a week I would be let out, and given ten minutes in which to shower, get my pencils sharpened, and anything else that had to be done. The rest of my time was spent inside that cell. Of course, I was hoping to be transferred in the very near future, which helped me to bear with it.

I was convicted of Escape, as were my four crime-partners, but this in no way affected my immediate position, as I still had to wait until the other case, in which I was to be a witness, came to trial, which was in July of 1969.

One other inmate also testified for the State in the Assault case—and was given a parole for it—but the victim, himself, would not; and the defendants were acquitted. At that time, I could not understand why the victim refused to testify against them, as he had admitted to me that the Mafia would still kill him if, and when, they got another chance at it; that he didn't hold to any "Convict's Code," so far as that went; and that he knew the State was really going to screw him around if he didn't testify. What he neglected to tell me, though, was that the State would screw him around a lot worse if he did testify. He had been in prison for about five years, and had done a good portion of that time in the Hole, so he was well acquainted with the way things worked in that respect. I had to find out for myself—the hard way.

After the trial, I was supposedly recommended for transfer to Sierra by both the District Attorney, and supposedly disapproved by Sacramento.

The most important thing in a case like this is to get the witness out of the institution as quickly as possible, as each day he has to spend there, the more inmates find out who he is; that he was a State's witness; and what he looks like. His number of enemies increase daily. Yet, 1970 rolled around and I was still in that same cell with no hope in sight. I was not awaiting transfer to anywhere. I guess you could say my status, at that time, was "Hold, pending miracle."

I made use of those many months in Solitary Confinement by studying; sometimes spending up to twelve and fourteen hours a day in my books, which were, for the most part, on Ancient, and Eastern Philosophy; Theology; and some poetry. (These books, incidentally, were sent in by my people, and were not obtained through any library facility here, to which I had no access.) My studies, more than anything else, carried me through those dark months. If it hadn't been for a hope, and belief, in "Universals," I would have cursed Life, Man, and God—and hung myself.

The degradation—the mental and emotional stress that I was put through—defy expression. I believe the law states that a man will not do more than twenty-nine days, at any one time, in Isolation. Yet, I did months and months in complete solitude; Solitary Confinement, in the true sense. This, not because of anything that I had done wrong, but because I had testified for the State.

I had my food thrown in my face and all over my cell. I had urine dumped in through my window from the cell above; and, even after cleaning it up, the smell would remain. One morning I poured my milk into my cup, as usual, only to find the bowl it had been served in covered with human feces. Day in and day out other inmates beat and kicked on my door, calling me every filthy name imaginable, and threatening to kill me, etc. Friends were afraid to even come near my door, as that would place their own lives in danger. And, because of flying objects, it got to the point where I dreaded coming out of my cell, even for my weekly shower.

Once, when I had been let out, an inmate, whose tray-flap happened to be open, shot me with a blow-gun (which is not an uncommon weapon in the Hole). The dart went over an inch and a half into my shoulder, and the officer who removed it had to really tug to get it out. Had this dart hit a more vital area, it would have been bad. As it was, it was bad enough that I decided I'd rather just stay in my cell.

Being in the A/C—regardless of the fact that mine was not a disciplinary case—brought more penalties than I can possibly list here. (All my crime-partners on the Escape—some of whom had bad records, and none of whom had a record as clean as mine—had long since been released from the Hole. I had total loss of privileges, just because I was housed in the A/C: That meant I could go to no movies, or watch T.V. I had no access to the Library, Chapel, Yard, or Gym. I could not work, or go to school; nor could I participate in any classes, groups, or social gatherings. I was not allowed to have my typewriter, guitar, stereo, hobby-crafts; not even my razor or hair brush. Many of the items sold in the canteen cannot be purchased by A/C inmates—some because of coming in glass or metal containers, but most are excluded for no good reason at all. So I had to do without them, also.

The food was a major issue in itself. During my time in the A/'C, I saw fried eggs scratched off the menu on account of getting cold before they could be served; then scrambled eggs were cut out for exactly the same reason. Now all they have are hard-boiled eggs—which are cold by the time they get served. That is just one example of the change for the worse. Another is steak: Whenever the mainline is enjoying steak or chops, the A/C is having veal, or some other rank substitute. The reason for this is that the steak bones can be made into lethal weapons. (Ballpoint pens with brass fillers, and toothbrushes with standard-length handles, were outlawed for the same reason: they can be used as weapons.)

I think the food was—and is—intentionally sabotaged in

order to impress on the minds of the inmates that the A/C
is not to be desired, but rather avoided (that is only the opinion
of a layman, of course). At any rate, it was messed up—and mine
even more so. All my meals were cold, as I was always served
last on account of the officer having to open my extra padlock
to give me my tray. Then, after having found feces in it, my ap-
petite seemed to become less and less, until I would almost get
sick just thinking about food.

There were many other A/C "hardships," of course, besides
the food. The amount of money a prisoner is allowed to draw
per month was—and still is—cut in half (to match the way in
which his selection of canteen items had been reduced, I guess).
Then, instead of three sets of clean clothes each week (as on the
mainline), I was fortunate to get one—and only by accident would
it be a set that fit. If my people came to see me, I would have to
go out to the visiting room looking like Bozo the clown, because
of ill-fitting clothes with paint and oil spots on them (due to the
fact that the A/C gets only work clothes—and the rejects, at
that).

Visits were another major issue. The visiting hours are from
10:00 am till 3:00 pm, daily. Yet, my people, after having driven
hundreds of miles to see me, would have to wait as much as two
hours, or more, for an officer escort to bring me to the visiting
room. (All A/C prisoners must be escorted everywhere they go.)
And this happened more times than I can remember. In addition
to losing that precious time, another forty-five minutes was cut
off the end of my visit, as with all others from the Hole, in order
to get me back to the A/C in time for supper—even though
I would have rather bought my supper from the vending machines
in the visiting room. Also, I was made to sit at a reserved table
right up front, under the watchful eye of the guard, instead of
being allowed to choose my own seating arrangement as is done
by mainline prisoners.

Small things like no fingernail clippers, and the way in which
toothbrush handles are broken off so short that a person can't

even brush his front teeth—perhaps they seem totally insignificant; but these are the things that make up the A/C life, which is more of a purgatory than anything else. It is, in fact, death on the installment plan. Each day a prisoner is tortured psychologically and spiritually (if there is really a difference), until, finally, he just leaps in one direction or the other. Maybe he will stab someone else for no reason at all: I've seen that. Or maybe he will take a razor blade and slice himself up from head to toe: I've seen that, too. Or, then again, maybe he will just hang himself like one fellow who lived a few doors away.

All these "small, insignificant things" cripple hundreds—thousands—of men for life. They will never be the same again. What they will be, though, are the "repeaters" that everyone talks about, who spend their lives in and out of prison. If they weren't criminals when they came here—and many are not—they are almost guaranteed to be by the time they have been through the "Vegetation Process" of this A/C—or the whole institution, for that matter.

As I was saying, I did months of it. Miserable time, that is. And not because of any wrong that I had done. I was punished for "Protection."

Then finally, in February—one year ago this month—after my having done eight straight months of Solitary Confinement, subjected to the above said abuse, I was approved for transfer to the Chino Guidance Center (a Medium-security institution), as a permanent work crew member. A week later, I was there.

The Chino work crew is housed in the honor wing; so I went directly to that wing upon my arrival. As for duties: I was assigned to the Medical Clinic, which is where I worked until being crated up and shipped back here.

Other than finding it difficult to converse with people, I got along fine. The months of solitude, which I had done here, made it hard for me to communicate with others. In fact, I had developed a slight speech impediment (or is that something one develops?). Here, in Solitary, I had gone, sometimes, as much as a week without even opening my mouth except to eat or brush my teeth, for lack of someone to talk to; and this was bound to take its toll. But, other than that, all went well.

Escape was not my intention. Had it been, I would not be here now writing this. Chino has no gun-tower manned at night; and any prisoner on the work crew there with a desire to run—he would be as good as gone. For that reason, of course, the crew members are selected with care, and no "escape risks" accepted. An exception to the rule seems to have been made in my case, thanks to a couple of people who had a bit of faith in me, and I was given the benefit of the doubt. Except for no contact visits, as enjoyed by the other crew members—which was strange, as I had had contact visits my whole time before—I was allowed full freedom and privileges. And, after having been in the Hole for over a year—fourteen months, to be exact—it was, for me, a veritable Utopia, which I did my best to enjoy. In my opinion, I also proved myself *not* to be an "escape risk" (and I never would have been one here, if life in this institution had been even halfway bearable). Had I intended to escape, I could have done so—and would have done so—my first day there.

I had been at Chino about six weeks when the Captain called me to his office one day and informed me that I was being locked up on account of a "rumor" which had reached him, that some inmates with knives were planning on killing me. He said I would have to be locked up in the Hole until this rumor could be checked out, and the inmates apprehended, if such inmates existed. Well, I never saw the Captain again, because I was on the next bus back to San Quentin. That was on April 1st; my having had a six-week "vacation."

Upon my return here, I was put straight back into an Isolation cell, with two additional locks and a bar on my door (sounds familiar, doesn't it?); and so began another stretch of "Punishment for Protection." At that time I had no idea how long it would be before I would be allowed to live like a human being. And I still have no idea how long it will be. It has been another ten months now, making a grand total of two years in this A/C (though I am presently in the hospital), and three years in this institution. There is no use in repeating all the above: suffice it to say that I have had to endure the same exact treatment as before.

Some months after my return, there was a major shift in A/C personnel here. A new Program Administrator and Counselors took over my unit, wreaking havoc and terror throughout for both inmates and officials (although the latter could hardly be expected to admit it publicly). However, I will try to keep my anathemas to a minimum.

One day the new P.A. came over to my unit and informed me that I should pack my stuff, as I was moving to another wing. I thought he had flipped out at first, but he was quite serious. My protests that I would not be safe in that wing, and that the inmate against whom I had testified was housed there, were futile. The P.A. said I was moving; no ifs, ands or buts. So I was forcefully —though not violently—escorted to this wing (I wanted it known, and on record, that the move was definitely against my will, as did another prisoner who protested in the same manner: by having to be forcefully escorted).

The first six cells of the third tier West had been screened off; and this special section was to be used for the Hi-power Protective cases, of which there were three at that time. Actually, however, that section was not nearly as safe as the other wing, where there had at least been a gun-rail and closed-front cells. The gate separating our section from the rest of the tier was flimsy enough that one or two inmates could have torn it down, using just their bare hands. And as for insulation against verbal abuse: there was none. The cells were open-front; the prisoner left open to any and all verbal harassment.

On top of that, it turned out that the inmate whom I had testified against was living almost directly below me, on the second tier—when he should not even have been in the same institution, let alone the same wing. Of course, he kept up a steady stream of threats and name-calling; agitating other inmates into joining in his daily—and nightly—tirade. Several times— nay, MANY times—I asked some other officials, up to, and in-

cluding the superintendent himself for a transfer to Chino-proper
(C.I.M.) or a camp—or at least a move out of that wing. It was
unnecessary for me to explain my reasons for such a request (although I did so each time), as he stood right there in front of
my cell, listening to the psychological harassment from the tier
below; and then had the audacity to tell me—over the din of
name-calling—that he felt I would be much happier there, once I
got used to it (he, not being well enough acquainted with my case
to know that I had spent six months there before).

Things became so miserable for me that I went on a hunger-
strike; the only non-violent way in which I could protest the cruel
treatment, and push for an alleviation. It was either that or tear
my sink and toilet off the wall, burn my mattress and bedding,
etc.—all of which is cause for disciplinary action, and an expense
to my people, whose money would be taken off my account to
pay for the destroyed property—and pad a few pockets, no doubt.

This hunger strike was in October of last year. After twenty-
one days (my having not been admitted to the hospital), an
interview was set up. Present were my uncle (Dan Nevis), who
flew down from Washington state; the attorney handling them
who did nothing the whole time but voice insults, and admit
how little they knew of my case. I, too, was there—in person.
The purpose of the meeting, supposedly, was to come to some
kind of agreement concerning a transfer, and my eating again.
Finally, after much discussion (my informing the Staff of things
they were already aware of, for the benefit of the others present),
it was agreed that if I began eating again, the Deputy Superintendent himself would place a phone call, that same day, to
the Superintendent of Chino Guidance Center, and arrange a
transfer for me back to the work crew there. So I began eating.
And the transfer was disapproved, on the grounds that the work
crew now lived in a dormitory, rather than individual cells (which
everyone knew before the interview, including myself). However,
one bit of new information did come out of the deal: I was informed that I had alienated certain inmates on the crew at Chino
when I had been there before. I had suspected my transfer back

to San Quentin was due to a certain inmate down there, when I had first been informed of the "rumor" about the inmates with knives—and even said as much—but there had been no way to confirm it until it came out during the course of our "negotiations."

The ex-Deputy D.A. who was prosecutor on my Robbery case is down there—or was at that time—and he has enough "connections" to get anyone transferred out (he is in there for murder, himself). And it stands to reason that he would feel a bit uncomfortable around someone whom he had prosecuted; especially to be incarcerated with him. I don't hold grudges—but he could hardly have known whether that was true or not. Anyway, under the cover of the "rumor," they could just ship me out without any further ado; no explanations, investigations, nothing. Nice and neat. But San Quentin was pleased with the outcome of the interview, for it had served its purpose from their point of view: I was eating again.

I endured that section of the wing for another two months, without protest other than letters written, etc; during that time, having my cell flooded, and being subjected to the greatest amount of discomfort due to smoke (the prisoners on the tier below were burning mattreses, bedding, and anything else that would burn, in protest of the way they, themselves, were being subjected to mistreatment, and "warehoused" in the A/C). Then, on the 22nd of December, I again went on "fast," and have not touched a meal to this day (February 15); almost two months.

For over two weeks the officials here ignored the fact that I was not eating (maybe thinking I was "fudging," by sneaking some food on the side). They also ignored my many requests for transfer to a Minimum-security institution, where I would be relatively safe, and, at the same time, be able to live like a man, instead of an animal. (In January, after my having done three years in prison, I became eligible for a Minimum custody transfer.)

Mr. H., a welcome visitor, came to see me on the 6th of January, and perhaps made a complaint with the Staff here about the way I was not eating, and the way in which nothing was being done for me. At any rate, the next day found me admitted to the hospital, where I am now typing this. I was admitted for "observation," and up till the 15th of the month, that is all they did: observe that I was not eating, and not going to. On that day they took action and fed me "intravenously"; and likewise the two days following. When I still would not eat, a tube was run up through my nose, down my throat, and into my stomach; and that is where it remained, twenty-four hours a day, for a week. By pouring liquids down this tube several times a day, they "force-fed" me.

The "I.V." had been bad enough, as they seemed to have difficulty getting my veins to stand up under the treatment. Several collapsed, which is painful; and, for a month afterward (which it is right now) my arms were yellow and purple blotched from the bruises under the surface. But when they stuck that tube in my nose and left it there, I thought I was going to die for sure. I don't know if that same process is so bad on the outside, but for me it was terrible.

I might also add that this sad condition was observed by two lawyers from Berkeley: Fay Stender, and Elaine Wender, who interviewed me concerning the cruelty I've been subjected to here (and both of whom have written to officials here in my behalf, formally requesting my transfer to a Minimum-security institution). It was, no doubt, evident that the "tube" routine was a rough way to go, as I could hardly speak, turn my head, or sit down (the reason for my difficulty in sitting down was not due to the tube, of course, which was in my nose and would not affect me where I sit down; but I had, since the 18th, been receiving vitamin shots—and they did affect me. Where I sit down). And having been unable to shave, I also had a five-day growth of garbage on my face; and, along with that, I had to wear my hospital clothes, which consisted of pajamas (green, size 96), and a shredded piece of terry-cloth that they tried to tell me was a bathrobe, when any fool could see that it was a towel. This is how I had to present myself to an attorney (who also happens to be an attractive woman) with whom I had never spoken before. I'm sure I felt every bit as miserable as I looked.

On the 25th, when I still hadn't relented, the tube was taken out of my nose—and put in my mouth instead, where it remained twenty-four hours a day, as before. A few days of that, and it was removed altogether. Now, three times a day, it goes down for my "force-feeding," and then comes out again (not by itself, of course). About half an hour before feeding time, a tray of food is brought into my room and left. If I dump it in the commode, I get credit for eating it—so I must leave it set where it is. And look at it. And smell it. And get my tube ready for the egg-nog-type concoction that they will pour into me.

For the past ten years, my weight had been between 140 and 145. The day I was admitted to the hospital it was 130. And, since that time, it has continued to drop—even though I am being force-fed. This morning—my fifty-fifth day without accepting a meal—I weighed 115½. Of course, I am quite skinny.

So it would appear that, eventually, if something is not done, my health will deteriorate completely. But that is the chance I must—and will—take. I would rather risk impairing my physical health, than to become a psychological cripple by remaining under the same conditions I have experienced over the past two years. Make that three years, as it was bad even on the mainline. Or make it four years, because the year in the L.A. County jail was almost as bad—and, in some ways, worse.

I have been warned, by both inmates and officials, of some of the possible repercussions I may suffer if I persist in making things difficult for the System: for instance, a transfer to Vacaville for treatment, where I would be housed in the Maximum-security wing (S-wing, I believe); and the possibility of having my mind altered by such processes as "Electro-shock therapy," or one of the many experimental drugs, such as Prolixin. This has happened to prisoners in the past.

On the other hand, I have also been told that if I just try to stick it out the way I have been—without eating—that I may be left right here indefinitely, as it is creating no problem for anyone. Either way, though it is preferable to the Hole, even if it is at the sacrifice of my meals—which I would enjoy eating. And I think I should add that the special section for Hi-power Protective Custody has been relocated. It is now, I understand, on the first tier, and even worse than the third tier. As this shift has taken place since I came to the hospital, I cannot state for sure the conditions; but another inmate, whom I know, could say for a fact, as he is there now.

There is much more that I could tell; more than will will ever be told, I think. What I have said here doesn't even begin to tell of the cruelty which I have suffered in this institution: all the many details, which slip more into the distance with each passing day. Things which, at first, seem so big; then, after a day or so, are almost forgotten. An example of that is my property:

The day I was brought to the hospital, I asked that my property be sent over as soon as possible, as inmates had been flooding the tiers, and with no one in my cell to get my stuff up off the floor (which is the only place A/C prisoners have to keep most of their things), it would be ruined. Day after day I asked for it to be brought over here, and each day was assured that it was on its way. Then, after two weeks had gone by, I was informed that the tier had been flooded, and much of my property destroyed: my books, photographs, letters, etc. In short, everything of value which I was allowed to have in the A/C. When I first heard it, it was big enough to cause earthquakes and tidal waves. I felt an extreme anger toward the negligence behind it, for which there could be no excuse. How do you replace a letter that has been written you sometime in the past? Or a photograph of someone you will never see or hear from again? You don't. When they're gone, they're gone forever. Yet, now when I think about it, it seems like something that happened a very long time ago in a far-away place; very unimportant.

But it should not be forgotten that easily. The APATHY that makes a prisoner's life a Hell. Yes, everywhere one turns, it is there. The officials don't care one way or the other: it is APATHY, pure and unadulterated. And occasionally Malice, of course, but that is only secondary. Don't take this to mean that there are NO officials who try to alleviate the suffering and madness which I have tried to tell a little about here; there ARE; and they DO try to alleviate it. But they are few and far between; and their power is extremely limited. And for them to stand behind something like what I've written here would be almost occupational suicide. For that reason, I expect nothing other than perhaps a whispered word of encouragement—which I have already received from a few different places.

Almost a year ago I wrote a story and got it smuggled out (along with my latest mug-shot). It was quite mild, in comparison with the awful reality—but it was enough that my people feared I would be killed, were it printed. Well, before it is all over, I may be—"accidentally," no doubt—but I will say what I have to say till then.

George F. Myron

at date of this printing this boy is under 100 lbs!—*his mother*

Folsom
June 22, 1971

Dear Fay:

The committee never says why they will not let me out [of the Adjustment Center] other than Lt. Campoy says he has too many of my kind out on the yard now which can mean anything and there is some sort of summary report from Soledad which according to this committee states that I am a revolutionary and agitator. I have never read this, but I must believe that something of the sort exists because out of sixteen who came on the bus I did from Soledad "O" Wing, I was the only one detained.

Other things were asked in the committee e.g. Was I writing you? Do I know so and so? and that it was Soledad's opinion that I could not make in on any main line. But these were never offered as reasons for keeping me.

Perhaps I have no room to cry, there are a few in this building with dates, who are not in Protective Custody, that they will not let out and there are more than a few who have far in excess of the time I have in A/C for charges not nearly as serious as what I am accused of, but it seems that they are just abusing their powers by doing any of us like this. It would make more sense if they found you guilty of a 115 and gave you a set penalty; if you don't pick up any more beefs while confined, either let you out or transfer you, but this indeterminate brutality of no other institution will take you and we don't think you are ready for here, come back in 30 days, in 90 days and we will see, and when you come back the same ignorant questions are asked, with the same damn results and all the time the board is creeping closer and we all know their thoughts on people who must appear from Adjustment Centers. Everyone is an undisputed God, but no-one is benevolent. The courts with their deliberate speed would not do justice to a snail. Southern prisons with their overt physical brutality are not nearly as insidious as this enlightened mental torture of everything being indeterminate, never ending, subject to whim, caprice, designed to destroy mind and soul, and even they admit, they don't know what they are doing, but they lie, they know all to well, destroy pride, strip integrity, murder a man's desire to think as an individual, to function with the mass, train him to watch and withstand brutality against self and kind without him raising a cry and you have a robot for the assembly lines, who out of fear can only identify with greed and corruption, who in a land of immense wealth will accept substandard education, pestilence, exploitation and who can not understand the fact that capitalistic oppression has no color lines, no ethnic demarcations, only rulers and the damned.

Is yours really a job in the conventional sense, Fay? I hope not; people soon tire of those things and eventually withdraw. This has to be a labor of love, a love of life, an involvement with humanity. I wrote this, I will be punished for it, I hate pain, but I would detest myself if I ceased to think or express the truth. It is personal now, those that would destroy me have the power to keep me physically caged, but that which is their primary goal, my spirit and mind must always beyond a doubt, but the I is many; more join the ranks daily. You must not only articulate, you must grasp, feel, become immersed in, you must live, and that is done by being humane and purposeful. I have preached this sermon to tell you of your many virtues.

As Always Yours,
Nolan

Folsom
August 26, 1970

Comrade Mine:

It is one in the morning and I cannot sleep. I owe you a letter but have been too filled with ugliness to write.

I would like a cup of coffee. I have all of the ingredients but hot water. A luxury I can't buy with a pack of cigarettes at one in the morning. Everyone is locked up. Even the pigs.

Hot water a luxury in America in 1970. Imagine that! Do you know how we get hot water? In a one gallon tumbler or can, poured through the bars at five o'clock in the morning. Everyone must drink or wash—or both—in this water at his own risk. Maybe the water cans have been poisoned by some nut; pissed in by a degenerate; spit in by the dude who brings it or someone who passed the night before. The five gallon cans in which we are brought water are left out on the tiers—they are not locked up or their cleanliness protected in any other way. I have seen men use them to soak their feet, wash their underwear and even use them to scrub their cells.

A bad scene? a dog's scene?

I would not drink the coffee I want so badly if someone would appear before my cell offering me hot water in one of those buckets. I have learned to wash in cold water, shave and do everything else in it. Hot water is a luxury here.

I am cold—it's freezing and they have the cold air blowing through the vent but then the black pig on the gun-rail and the white one on the floor both have heaters and hot water.

The bitch HATE shakes my cup before my eyes, her warm arms around my neck and whispers in my ear.

I must get in bed and try to think of you.

Take care.

All Power To The People
Nadifu

December '70
San Quentin

Dear ————,

The days and months that a guard has to spend on the ground (sometimes locked in a wing or cell-block with no gun guard) are what destroy anything at all that was good, healthy, or social about him before. Fear begets fear. And we come out with two groups of schizoids, one guarding the other. The spiral extends outward and up.

At first hint of reluctance to aid them in your own corruption, you'll bring down on your head anything from pick-handles to panic-stricken gunfire.

All pretenses and disguises are abandoned; the guard is there to hold you, there is no need for him to fake the idea that he is a public servant. He is there to kill you if you touch the wall or resist his heavy hand too strongly. Reducing men to trembling and dormancy is his trade. There is no other method to hold a man inside an American prison. Consider now that anyone who has handled guns knows they are far from perfect tools.

Terror becomes an absolute necessity. The wall is thus given a symbolic fatal quality of its own; the wall and barbed wire fences must never even be touched. Lines are painted in front of them, a misstep across this line could bring the blow that kills. Even if no one dies the fact of being shot at for so small an indiscretion has a permanent effect on all who witness it.

George L. Jackson

Soledad
January 1971

Dear Mrs. Stender:

The prison system—once entered—*will* change a man. But in what way, is determined not so much by the man, but by the new world that the man enters, the one that is based on illiteracy, violence, mass confusion, and a constant non-qualitative busyness that limits to the utmost; confrontation with reality. The convicts say, "We have nothing to do in here," to this, I say it is only partially correct, for we have nothing that is "Qualitative" to do in here, the officials know this—and they enjoy this also. There is always a card game (illegal), a crap game (illegal), a sports pool (illegal), a domino game, a fight (illegal), or two men committing sodomy (illegal), a killing (illegal), and the continuous vigilent make up of each man (some are so geared up until paranoia is inevitable), the frame of mind has one intrinsic thought: Stay Alive.

Sincerely,
John I. Spain

Soledad
Feb. 22, 1971

Dear Sister Fay,

Well today the people came who you had told me about but the Pigs knew about it a little too early because about 15 to 20 minutes before the People and Dr. Rundel were here they turned our water on to try and clean things up a little. But I feel they saw enough because all we had in our rooms were one blanket and a sheet, legal paper and a few other things that I had gotten us from the canteen. They saw boxes and boxes full of garbage all along between our cells and us only in shorts and a tee shirt. What's funny about it is that we have only had a mattress two whole days since the first of February: one time when Dr. Rundel came to see us, and that was given to us about one hour before and then again on the first few minutes of this visit . . .

Fay, when I see you I've got to say much more but mostly to thank you for giving people the chance to see it as it really was. Keep your head up and stand tall. We are no matter what,

Yours Very Truly,
Mr. Raymond Marquez

The Sergeant and the Gold Watch

Dear Mrs. Stender:

I just received a letter from Mr. G. at Folsom. First of all I have been knowing Sgt. P. since 1966 and I know for a fact that I gave him my watch. I told him it had been reported stolen but had been recovered two days before I went to A.C.

Sgt. P. is the same one that I told you about who threatened me about the Soledad incident. And you don't mistake anyone with him because he weighs about 300 pounds.

I told him that my watch had been reported stolen and he said he would notify R&R and inform them that I had recovered it. Nothing I had on me the day I was put in A.C. has been received here. Which was my watch, wallet, and gold chain & medal.

Sgt. P. has given other inmates property to inmates he favors and one of these inmates came to Chino with me. He worked for Sgt. P. in A.C. and told me about it.

But I know beyond all doubt that it was Sgt. P. who took my watch from me, and that he was there in A.C. when I got there. On July 20, 1970. I guess I can kiss that good-by, but it just shows you why convicts kill these pigs. Because they have no morals or sense of justice and steal from us and there is nothing we can do about it.

Thank You for your assistance as I do appreciate it. But these people are pros so you know a convicts word isn't worth anything. I asked an inmate here to write you a letter explaining about Sgt. P. giving inmates property away.

"Very Sincerely Yours"
Gary

Chino
Aug. 31, 1970

Dear Mrs. Stender,

I'm writing in behalf of Gary Francisco. I was a worker in the Adjustment Center when I had the occasion to observe one Correctional Sgt. P. abuse the property of Gary Francisco.

The following items listed were disposed of in the following manner:

(1) one gold wrist watch with a gold expansion band was given to St. P.'s Informant. An unusual amount of toilet articles and other commissary items were given to the same person by Sgt. P.

Sgt. P. advised me to forget that I had seen the above transaction take place, and further offered me the pick of any further property of Gary Francisco which I might want, but I refused.

I also had the occasion to observe the abuse of other prisoners personal property by the same Sgt. P.

If you desire to take litigation by way of the court I will be more than willing to testify under oath what I have written.

I declare under oath of Perjury that the foregoing is a true and correct statement.

Dated: August 31, 1970:

Robert Donald LaBlue

Chino
Sept. 1970

Dear Fay,

My name is David E. Russell and I'm presently imprisoned at Palm Hall in Chino Calif. I'm a friend of Garry Francisco

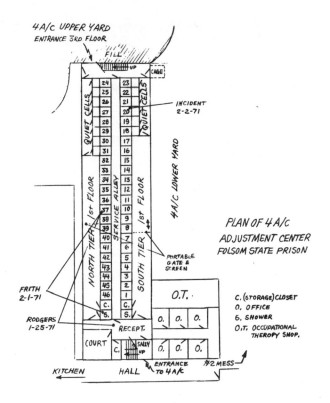

4 A/c UPPER YARD
ENTRANCE 3RD FLOOR

FILL

UP

CAGE

24	23
25	22
26	21
27	20
28	19
29	18
30	17
31	16
32	15
33	14
34	13
35	12
36	11
37	10
38	9
39	8
40	7
41	6
42	5
43	4
44	3
45	2
46	1
C.	C.
S.	S.

QUIET CELLS

QUIET CELLS

INCIDENT 2-2-71

4 A/C LOWER YARD

NORTH TIER 1st FLOOR

SERVICE ALLEY

SOUTH TIER 1st FLOOR

PORTABLE GATE & SCREEN

FRITH 2-1-71

RODGERS 1-25-71

O.T.

O. O. O.

RECEPT.

COURT

C.

SALLY UP

O. O. O.

KITCHEN

HALL

ENTRANCE TO 4 A/c

#2 MESS

PLAN OF 4 A/c
ADJUSTMENT CENTER
FOLSOM STATE PRISON

C. (STORAGE) CLOSET
O. OFFICE
6. SHOWER
O.T. OCCUPATIONAL THERAPY SHOP.

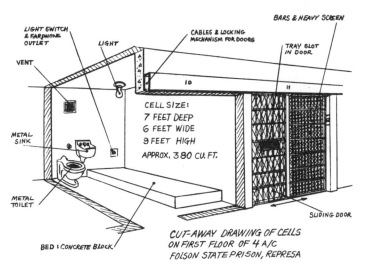

LIGHT SWITCH & EARPHONE OUTLET

LIGHT

CABLES & LOCKING MECHANISM FOR DOORS

BARS & HEAVY SCREEN

TRAY SLOT IN DOOR

VENT

10

11

METAL SINK

CELL SIZE:
7 FEET DEEP
6 FEET WIDE
9 FEET HIGH
APPROX. 380 CU. FT.

METAL TOILET

SLIDING DOOR

BED : CONCRETE BLOCK

CUT-AWAY DRAWING OF CELLS
ON FIRST FLOOR OF 4 A/c
FOLSON STATE PRISON, REPRESA

and would like to inform you that these cops down here are messing over him.

He tried to get a writ notarized and his counselor Mr. A. told him that Garry did not have any right to file any writ on civil rights or whatever he was filing. The counselor told Garry to give him the writ, Garry told him he wasn't going to take it. The counselor called four or five other cops over and said to Garry. "You're either going to give it to me or we're going to take it from you." Then the Big Wheel came out and Garry gave it to him.

Now they took Garry's job, put his cell on dead lock and wrote him up. His counselor doesn't like him or Don La Blue or any of us which hangs around together. These punks told me one time I better pick some new friends or else. Me and Garry just like brothers to each other and these cops don't like that too much. I don't like what there doing to Garry and know you can help out.

Garry's Friend
David E. Russell

Please excuse the handwriting Fay, I'm a little nervous.

David

Chino
Sept. 16, 1970

Dear Mrs. Stender:

Today I talked to Mr. G. at Folsom and he informed me that Sgt. P. admitted taking my watch, wallet, chain & medal.

They were unable to locate any of these things but Mr. G. said he would personally send me a replacement for my watch and wallet.

Thank you for your assistance. I'm sure they would have never admitted this if it had not been for you. They used this same policy at Soledad when they took my guitar and watch there. But I doubt if there is anyway to make them replace it. So its a loss.

Thank you again for helping me. What should I do if they take La Blue back to Folsom behind that letter? It's not beyond them. And he seemed a little concerned because he has had trouble with that Sgt. also.

I told him not to worry about it because if they did anything to him or attempted to that it would expose them. Also that I didn't think they would try because of the fact you have knowledge of the affidavit against that Sgt.

At any rate they are replacing part of my property. If anything comes up I'll let you know.

Gary Francisco

Chino
Sept. 17, 1970

Dear Mrs. Stender,

The verified affidavit that I sent to you in regards to Gary Francisco's property, evidently helped as Gary informed me today that Mr. G. was returning the property.

However I must let you know that if for any reason I'm returned to Folsom I won't ever be allowed to leave alive. The reason I'm telling you this is because the Administration at Folsom is so corrupt that it does all kinds of unlawful things, such as assaults and in some cases murder.

I'm extremely pleased that I was able to help you and Gary get his property restored to him.

Very Truly Yours
Robert D. LaBlue

Soledad
Oct. 20

Dear Mrs. Stender:

You cannot rehabilitate a man through brutality and disrespect. Regardless of the crime a man may commit, he is still a human being and has feelings. And the main reason most inmates in prison today disrespect their keepers, is because they themselves (the inmates) are disrespected and are not treated like human beings. I myself have witnessed brutal attacks upon inmates and have suffered a few myself, uncalled for. I can understand a guard or guards restraining an inmate if he becomes violent. But many a time this restraining has turned into a brutal beating. Does this type of treatment bring about respect or rehabilitation? No! It only instills hostility and causes alienation towards the prison officials from the inmate or inmates involved.

If you treat a man like an animal, then you must expect him to act like one. For every action, there is a reaction. This is only human nature. And in order for an inmate to act like a human being, you must treat him as such. Treating him like an animal will only get negative results from him. You can't spit in his face and expect him to smile and say thank you. I have seen this happen also. There is a large gap between the inmate and prison officials. And it will continue to grow until the prison officials learn that an inmate is no different then them, only in the sense that he has broken a law. He still has feelings, and he's still a human being. And until the big wheels in Sacramento and the personnel inside the prisons start practicing rehabilitation, and stop practicing zoology, then they can expect continuous chaos and trouble between inmates and officials.

Lewis Moore

In early 1970, a series of beatings took place in the Adjustment
Center at Folsom. A prisoner wrote these descriptions; his reports
were confirmed by attorneys' interviews and many other letters.

Folsom

January 26, 1971

Dear Sisters & Brothers,

On January 25, 1971, Don Rud, a Black inmate was brutalized by prison staff. He was beaten with a club while his hands were handcuffed behind his back. The facts are as follows:

Don Rud is confined in Folsom State Prison under the protection of the law, under the care and in the custody of the California Department of Corrections.

Rud had been taken to the Board Room in the Administration BLD. of Folsom State Prison on the morning of January 25, 1971, for his annual appearance before the California Adult Authority. I understand there was a Hearty Exchange of words, Rud being a Macrologist and somewhat of a fool in my personal opinion.

Be that as it may, he isn't a Militant Black, he's more the Uncle Tom, cap-in-hand-type Black Buck, who believes whatever the Administration tells him. His Chatter is the only thing which gets him in trouble, that and his homosexual activities. In my opinion he should be restrained in a mental institution where his problems could be better treated.

I became aware at approximately 2 o'clock on the afternoon of January 25, 1971, that someone had come into the reception area of the Adjustment Center from the Sally Port Area, when the sound of a key in a lock was followed by the slam of the heavy doors which close 4A off from the rest of the prison.

I recognized the sounds made by chains and handcuffs being removed from someone in the reception area. I heard the voice of the prisoner Don Rud talking with an officer as they stripped him down for the routine search every inmate receives when being returned.

I heard the sound of squeaks made by the metal detector and realized from personal experience that the officers were running it over the inmate's naked body as they visually searched for anything that the prisoner might have concealed in his mouth, hair, or other recesses of his body. Again I heard the handcuffs being replaced as they clicked shut. Then I heard the rustle of papers and knew from the many times I'd gone to the Board and out that the officers were now searching the Legal Material carried by the inmate. This was confirmed a few moments later when I heard one of the officers say: "Leave one of the envelopes here." I heard the inmate very respectfully explain that the envelope contained Legal Papers he was using in his case, but the officer insisted, as if trying to provoke an argument, that he leave them.

There after, I heard the prisoner reply: "You're not taking my legal papers? I have a right to keep them with me." (Note: in 1969, the California Legislature Revised Penal Code Section 2600, and prohibited Prison Officials from taking or destroying a prisoner's legal material.)

At this, I heard the officer's voice become raised, as he yelled: "Give me that envelope, Nigger." I noticed the prisoner's voice take on a tone of fear as he replied: "I'm not going to fight you." It was apparent to me that Rud was being surrounded and force was about to be used on him. Having witnessed many attacks on inmates, I could sense in the air what was about to happen and instinctively jumped up and looked out my door to get a better view of the action. I could now hear the unmistakable sound of a club as it thundered on the bare body of the defenseless prisoner:

"Thud, Thud, Thud."

I heard the Prisoner's first cry of pain, followed by his pleading for the officers to stop their attack, as blow after blow was struck, the sound of the club echoing down the tier. "Thud, Thud, Thud." Then I became aware of other officers joining in on the attack as I heard the prisoner strangling, knowing that someone had him by the neck. The blows continued to be belted out, and above the cries of human suffering I could hear other inmates helplessly crying out of their cells to "Leave the man alone." Over this I could hear also the jeering voice of one officer hissing:

"Had enough, Nigger? Had enough?"

The struggle didn't stop as I knew they had their victim on the floor and were probably kicking in his ribs as I have seen them do on many occasions.

I heard more clubbing as the sound of the handcuffs were again clicking and I knew they were being tightened tighter on his wrists, and must be now cutting into the flesh. I heard the prisoner's last cry of pain which died out in one last gag and all was quiet.

It was about a minute later that the gate between the reception area and the tier was opened and I got my first good look at the battered and bruised body of the Black Buck with his hands still handcuffed behind his back being shoved by officers M., A., and L. under the supervision of W. and Officer L. M.T.A. H. stood by the gate as the voice of Correctional Counselor B. screamed orders to lock him up. Each of the officers passed close in front of my cell, and I got a good look at the hatred which filled their faces. I watched as they pushed Rud's bent frame, still handcuffed, into cell 37 and onto the hard concrete floor.

The silence was broken as I heard the cell door slam shut with a final "clang." I watched as Officer A. replaced the club he was waving back into his back pockets. Officers M. and L. moved on down the tier to the strip cells in the back and removed one of the other prisoners, so as to make room for Rud. As I look back over what had just transpired I recognized that during the entire struggle I didn't hear a word of profanity uttered from Rud, as might be heard from the more Militant Blacks we have here in 4A. But as I said before, Rud took treatment of this type as normal and maybe even right. And that moment the immediate pain was gone, and in the coming days I feel he'll be rationalizing it after the body heals, and he begins to talk.

Everyone of the tier felt every blow, and most are mad because Rud hasn't taken a more militant stance. I guess it's now his nature, being broken to the plow so to speak, to be as he is. This of course makes the more sane blacks become more angry, because they can see themselves in Rud and do not desire to submit to such Dehumanization.

I have written an affidavit to all this and filed two copies with the Superior Court with a complaint against the officers in question. I sent another to R. K. Procunier, Director of Corrections, in a hope that he'll move to clean up Folsom and implement long needed reforms. I will also write the Legislature, for I feel that Folsom may very well soon explode into violence if this oppression and inhumanity is not stopped. I hope you'll read this letter to as many people as you can so they can realize the hopeless situation we prisoners find ourselves in.

All Power to the People
Your Brother In Peace
Harold Williams Olson

Folsom
February 1, 1971

Dear Brothers and Sisters,

On January 8th, 1971, we had an attack on Johnny Brandon. On January 25th, 1971, I reported the beating administered to Don Rud. Today, I'm sorry to report another act of brutality.

The situation in the 4 A/C Adjustment Center is becoming

very dangerous, but I feel someone must communicate the news.

The day following the incident involving Rud, a fellow known to me as Wally Frith was brought into 4 A/C and placed in Rud's vacated cell. Rud had been moved back into a strip cell and cell 37 was left open. I live in cell 46 at the front end of the tier.

Frith is about 5 foot 10 inches, weight about 135 pounds, slender with red hair and a walrus mustache. He looks and sounds like Wally Cox, if Mr. Peepers had a mustache. I'm sure he couldn't lick his way out of a bag of marshmellows. It's hard to tell his age, but I'd say he's in his late 40's or early 50's although I can't see any gray hair. In short, he's just a scrabby old man, mean maybe, but not much to be afraid of, unarmed.

At about 7:30 o'clock in the A.M. of February 1st, 1971, three Correctional Officers passed my cell (cell 46) moving east and stopped in front of cell 37 of the 4 A/C adjustment Center. They waited a minute and Officer L., the second watch officer in charge of the first floor, cranked open the cell door from controls at the west end of the tier.

I watched out my door, as the three officers entered cell 37. A second later I heard a commotion, like the sound of a brawl. I have no idea of what provoked the brawl, other than to say that I didn't hear the officers call Frith out of his cell or hear Frith say anything to the officers. It appeared to me that the three officers intended to enter the cell from the time they entered the tier. The gate on the tier was left opened, which is unusual and the second the sound of the brawl reached my ears, two more officers came running down the tier. Officer L. remained at the gate and closed it only after these last two guards had entered the tier.

The officers in Frith's cell were A., O., and a new colored officer I'd never seen before. The two officers running down the tier were B. and another officer I don't recognize. Just as the two officers reached the front of cell 37, Frith came flying out. I mean literally, as if he had been thrown. He was picked up by B. and the other and carried past my cell to the shower stall between my cell and the gate where Officer L. stood. Frith was shoved into the shower stall and Officer B. followed him in carrying a heavy brass key in his fist.

The keys used at Folsom are about one inch wide and six or seven inches long. They're about a quarter of an inch thick and in a fight, they're as good as any pair of brass knuckles.

After the brawl began again, I heard Frith begin to strangle and saw his feet sticking out of the shower stall. The other four officers moved in like a pack of wolves and began punching and kicking their victim.

Unlike Rud, Frith was not handcuffed, he didn't have to be, for the reasons I've already stated. The five officers combined weight is close to half a ton. Frith didn't have a chance. He was strangled, beat, and kicked until the sadistic urge in the officers had been satisfied. Like Rud, he was placed in a strip cell (26) and a fraudulent report was written on him, to justify the assault.

All Power To The People
Your Brother In Peace
Harold William Olsen

Folsom
February 3, 1971

Dear Brothers And Sisters:

Today was shower day in 4 A/C and I watched with interest as they brought Wally Frith past my cell. He has one very black eye, a cut on his nose and numerous other marks. Other than that, he's lucky to be able to walk, because I saw how they kicked him.

Yesterday, while the action was going on in the strip cells, I noticed the pigs open all the windows. I didn't think anything about it, and then my eyes began to run tears. I thought maybe I'd got something in them, and so I washed them out with cold water. I must of been slow, because it was quite awhile before I realized that the pigs had shot tear gas into the strip cells after-wards and had locked the doors sealing it in on their victims. It's been sometime since I saw them last use tear gas or mace, and not hearing anything more than a few cries, I was a bit surprised. With all the windows open between my cell, number one, and the strip cells, I got enough to irritate my eyes.

All Power To The People
Your Brother In Peace
Harold William Olsen

Folsom
December, 1970

Dear Mrs. Stender:

I am writing this letter to inform you that today a brother was throw in a hole. He went to the pig committee today. I don't know what was say, but when he came he sat fire to his cell, the brother is sick in the mind and need to be in the hospital, he need help. The pig turn the waterhose on him in his cell, then put him in the hole without a mattress or blankets. He can not read or write and the pig know it, his name is Benjamin B———

I feel that the years of oppression has did the brother mind in and someone need to help him. If here is anything that can be did for him, it will be appreciated by anyone here.

Right on
Tippy Williams

CMC East
December 6, 1970

Dear Fay and Patti:

There is an inertia and stolidity which is maddening even to the icy emotionless eyes of the more-or-less professional convict—the prison raised men who have made California prisons their only home. For instance, take myself. I was taken out of whatever good I *was* doing for myself at Folsom (three college courses and writing for the *Observer*) and am now placed in the kitchen as a food server. The few functioning programs in education here are designed to meet the need of the institution rather than the individual needs of its members. The demands of the prison managers are met and exercised by the guards, who, as you know, are not notably flexible men.

But men here carry the key to their cells (big thing!) and they are kept on pills of some sort, at least the most bothersome— called being "blindfolded" by most of the men. Well, I don't have a blindfold yet. I want to remember these places better than any man ever leaving here.

Yours,
Jim Williamson

Jamestown
November 24, 1970

Dear Mrs. Stender;

I am an inmate at the California Conservation Center of Jamestown, California. Sunday night Nov. 22, my wife was approached by a member of the staff here under a false pretense and using my name to get to her. He then bragged of his position here. He stated that he was first in authority and that he would make things bad for me. My wife is now so shook up that she is afraid to come here and visit and she is under a mental stress for fear I will be attacked by someone he has put up to it. If this person is so sick that he will prey on some one like a helpless woman I sure wonder just how sick he can be. His first call came at 1:00 in the morning after he called all over town to find out where she was staying. He could not get the Motel Manager to give him her room number so he hung up mad. He then called back about 15 minutes later saying he was me and must talk with my wife. Well there were no phones in the rooms so the Motel Manager had to get up and go get my wife. He then told here he was the Doctor who had just operated on me, for I was in the hospital. My wife was so scared she did not know what to do so she denied him the right to come to her room. He then asked her to meet him at the Bowling Alley she refused this and again he said it was urgent and he should talk with her, out of her fear that I was worse she agreed to see him at the cafeteria where she was staying because it was always full of people. She also told the Motel Manager all about what took place on the phone and told him to call if she did not return safely. After meeting him and talking for some 2 hours without being able to get away he asked when she would be back up here again. He then told her that he didn't want her to say anything about this to anyone because he could cause me a lot of trouble over it if she said anything. She is so scared he will try to do something to her now, that I am very worried and she does not want to come back here to visit.

Is there something that can be done about this? I am short of funds and could only pay you if a Law Suit is awarded in sums of money. I think it is a shame though that a man must pay such a price for being a prisoner that he should have to be subjected to such a thing by sick people who work here for the Dept. of Corrections. I do not know whether he will approach me now or not over my wife and I bringing him and his actions out in the light. I mostly hate to lose my visits and the worry for my wife is all uncalled for.

The person who did this thing is a Medical Training Assistant here, his name is Ronald J. He was drinking very heavily and he admitted it. (The Motel Manager will also witness as to his getting her out of bed on both phone calls.) He is still on the job here also, so apparently the Dept. is not going to do anything about his actions. If you can help I would be so grateful for it would mean a great deal to many inmates here and myself and my wife. The inmates are afraid he might do more next time and that their wifes might be next. I can't blame them for such things are a disgrace.

Thank You, for any assistance you may give,
Yours Truly,
(Name withheld by request)

This is an exact reproduction of a note written by Lieutenant Flores of the staff of Soledad Prison which he wrote in response to a request to see a doctor made by the author of the following letter.

> Jell for help
> when the blood is
> one inch thick
> all over the floor.
> Don't call before
> that.

San Luis Obispo
February 9, 1971

Dear Mrs. Fay:

I would like for you to file, and represent me in a Civil Action against the State of California. I will briefly explain it to you. On Jan. 29th, 1971, at 11:00 P.M. I got violently sick and vomit blood, I had one fellow inmate on this tier to call the police officer that was in charge of this third floor. When the police officer approached my cell I told him what had happened. He said he must get Sergeant D. before he could do anything and he did, and Sergeant D. escorted me to the hospital and then after reaching the hospital I had to wait for approximately 15 minutes before the M.T.A. saw me. I explained to the M.T.A. that I was throwing up blood, and he told me to wait a minute which turned into a 15 minute wait, he brought back with him two cops and asked me to throw up some blood in one of the cups which I did. Then he (M.T.A.) gave me two "pain pills," which I took and sent me back to my cell, and on the way back I throwed up more blood. After entering my cell I got upon my upper bunk and dozed off to sleep, and only to suddenly awaken choking. The blood was coming up again, I got off of the upper bunk in order to go to the toilet and before I could get to the toilet the blood came up, I then sat down on the toilet because I felt like I had to (defecate) which turned out to be blood instead coming out of my rectum, and I called over to the man in the next cell to call the police officer that was in charge, which he did along with other inmates taking up the calling of the officer, which he (officer) finally came to my cell and saw all of the blood on the floor and told me to put my clothes on and stand by the door which I did. At that time it was about 12:00 A.M. The officer left and I called over to the man in the next cell and gave him my mother's address and told him that I don't think I will make it because I am losing too much blood and I was "passing out." Four long miserable hours later I heard my cell door opening and felt myself being lifted to my feet and walked down that forever seemingly hall and stairs to a wheel chair, and I then passed out completely, the next thing I remember is awakening in the hospital with a needle in my arm, and having the third pint of blood pumped into me.

Mrs. Fay, it is the policy here that when someone is sick the Institution's ambulance to come and pick up the sick, and it is well equipped to get a person to the hospital fast, why why did they take so long before taking me to the hospital and why didn't they use a ambulance instead of a wheel chair? Could it be because I written to you in concern of this conspiracy that the staff got going against me and others?

Mrs. Fay, I written you a letter in 1970, and asked you for your assistance and you did help, but now I am in need of your assistance again because I must file "Civil Action" against this department and if you can help me please come to visit with me because I have a great deal more information I would like to discuss, or will you have someone from your firm to come? Either way Please write back at your earliest and let me know whether or not you can be of any assistance.

Respectfully Yours,
Arthur Lee Johnson

Statement of Facts

June 18th 1968, I arrived at Chino Guidance Center due to a thirty-six dollar check in which I pleaded guilty to forging. At El Centro Calif. At this time, I had very recently went under surgery for two herniers stemming from bowel troubles, the herniers was suspected by the doctors to possibly be causing the troubles with my bowels, prior to the hernia operation I had also had surgery on my right arm, both operations at this time mentioned (June 18th 1968) was still in the process of healing, and was given me troubles at all times, at this time the doctors at Chino some how over looked my condition, and in their classifying me, I was classified for Sierra Conservation Center to take fire fighting training which consisted of rugged, and hard type labor, which I was in no physical condition to do. When I arrived at Sierra the officials, and the doctors was very angry at me. After examining me and seeing my condition, I was told by the doctor that I was in the wrong place, and that I should not have come here, I tried to explain that I did not ask to come there, and that I was placed on the bus with other inmates, with no knowledge of where I was going. My trying to explain did no good, I was constantly harrassed about coming there. However the doctor disqualified me for the fire training, and assigned me to the kitchen. The using of my arm, caused it to swell so badly that the doctor took me out of the kitchen and placed me on Medicaly Unasigned. The operation on my stomach was also swelling and paining, I also was suffering so badly that I had no

other choice but turn to the court for help. So while I was unasigned I started preparing me a writ in an attempt to obtain
my medicine. On August 20th, 1968, I was called to the culinary
to work, although I was still on the doctors medical unasign lay in
I reported to the officer in charge and told him that I was medicaly unassigned, and that I had went through operation on my
stomach and arm, and at the time I was unable to perform my
dutys, he (the officer) says to me, it's not a damn thing wrong
with you, you just want to gold brick, you came to the wrong
place, for that, and you are going to work, or to the hole I
warned him that he was not the doctor, and that I would file
charges on him if they mistreated me in any way, he (the officer)
then stated, I would like to see the day that one convict win in
court over all of us; He then asked me if I was going to work;
I said I was going back to my barecks, and turned to leave, then
three officers grabbed me by my arms and said, not that way
boy, this way to the hole. Then I was placed in the hole on
concrete. When I was called to Prison Court, Mr. T., the Assistant
Warden asked me, Fartheree what is the matter with you? I have
a report here from the officers saying that you refused to work,
and cursed them, calling them predjudice son of bitches is this
so? I told him that these reports was false, and that I had cursed
no one. And furthermore I was medically unassigned, and that
they no right to try and work me. Mr. T. then asked the officer
is this so that he is medically unassigned? The officer stated he
didn't know, Mr. T. then instructed the officer to get my medical
file, and the doctor, when they got my file and doctor, the
doctor stated, yes, he is unassigned medically. Then Mr. T.
asked, who put a go to work notice on him; Someone has put
one in his jacket, then one of the officers told him that the yard
crew officer, Mr. M. did it he (Mr. T.), sent for Mr. M. and
asked him, did you put a go to work slip in Fartheree's jacket?
Mr. M. said he did, Mr. T. then told him that he had no right to
tamper with my medical file. Mr. M. then said, he had obtained
permission from someone that worked in the hospital, this was
someone other than the doctor, and no one has the right to do

this but the doctor. Mr. T. then told me, (I suspected in order to cover up), I am going to let you off light, since this was a mistake, otherwise, you would get no less than 15 days in the hole, consider yourself lucky that I am giving you only two days. I then said to him, while I am here I might as well mention that the doctors have taken my medicine, and have refused to give me any, and due to this I am preparing a writ to go into court to try and get my medicine. I also mentioned to Mr. T. that if in some way he could persuade them to give me my medicine I would not have to go to court. Mr. T. asked me when was I planning on sending my writ in? I said real soon. Mr. T. then stated that, this is the doctor's business about medicine, and I don't bother into it, he then added, but you will find yourself getting along a lot better here, if you don't try to be a smart con. I stated that I didn't mean to be smart, but I need my medicine very badly, and since it is refused to be given to me, I have no other choice but turn to the aid of the court. Mr. T. then ordered me carried to the hole. Upon my arrival at the hole I was placed in a cell that had nothing to lay on except a concrete slab and concrete floor. Even tho I was swollen and paining, I did my two days in the hole and was released. The concrete had swollen me worst than I was already, I had difficulties walking for several days. The doctor still left me on my medically unassigned, so I finished my writ and mailed it in on, or around, Aug., 28th 1968 then in Sept., 1968, I received a copy from the court of the order to show cause served on the doctor. Shortly after the doctor called me into his office, he was angry, and bawled me out for causing him to have to go to court, I told him that I had no other choice since he refused me my medicine. He then said, do you expect me to do anything for you when you are taking me to court? If I did you like that would you do anything for me? Then on, or around, Sept. 13th 1968, I was called to a small office, the man whom I was called to see introduced himself as Dr. H., a psychiatrist. He asked me did I know his purpose of seeing me? I told him that I did not know what he came to see me about, but, I did know that a psychiatrist job was to evaluate ones mental capacity,

so I could only assume that this was his purpose, he then asked
if I knew the date? I said yes, the 13th of Sept., he then asked,
what happened between you and the officers here? I explained to
him that while on a medical layin by the doctor, I had been called
to the kitchen to work, when I reported, and tried to explain that
I was medically unassigned due to operations on my arm and
stomach, I was ordered by the kitchen officials to go to work, or
to the hole, and being disable for work was the cause of the incident which occured. Then he asked, what about that writ you
sent to the court? What happened to cause that? I told him (Dr.
H.) how my medicine had been taken away by the doctor, and
that this was the purpose of the writ, he then asked, do you have
a copy of the writ? I said yes, so I went to the dorm and got it for
him. He read it, after reading it he then said that will be all.
About two hours after some officers came to my dorm and said,
up on your feet bum, it's back to the hole for you, then I was
taken to the same hole as before, and placed on bare concrete,
there I remained until I was carried to court. I asked several
times to see a doctor and was refused each time. When I arrived
at court, Dr. L. (Chief M.D. Officer), tried to convince the
judge that I was mentally ill, by producing the phony psyc charge,
made out by Dr. H. Although my writ was filed in court in an
attempt to get my badly needed medicine now the doctors was
attempting to make my case look as though I was an extremely
dangerous mental subject of some kind, and that this being the
true cause of our troubles at the center. But the judge could sense
what they were doing, and he (the judge) made it very clear to
them, that he suspected them to be using the psyc report as a
defense against my charges, the judge also mentioned to them
that the psyc Dr. H., had gone a long way out of his way to make
the psyc charge against me, by making certain statements from
my past record which had no bearings at all in a mental report,
other than a defence against my charges. When the judge asked
why I was placed in a place of punishment, and was this did
because of me writing my writ? They attempted to have the judge
believe that they placed me in a holdover, due to the Report

so as to wait the out come of court. But they did not place me in a holdover cell, a holdover cell has a bed, blankets, towels, and warm water, I was placed in the hold where men are put for punishment with nothing to lay on but concrete, with nothing to cover with. These things were brought out in court, and admitted by the prison officials at court. I am submitting my court results as evidence, and placing it on the bottom of my statement of facts. After court I was brought back to the center, and placed back in the hold. I asked the officer in charge, is this where they are going to keep me? I thought the judge told them to put me in a regular cell, and take me out of the hold. The officer stated, you should have stayed in the judge's chamber because he don't run this in here. Then the officer asked, do you think you bettered yourself any by going to court? I said yes, I will be leaving here away from these people and maybe I'll get my medicine where I am going. The officer then said, boy we got people where you are going, and these jackets we hook you up to, the people where ever you go pick them up. Where we leave off at, you will see.

When I arrived at Vacaville Medical Center, the Psyc Doctor there had an interview with me to test my mental stability, when he was finished, he told me, that the Dr. [at the camp] had sent me to Vacaville on a Cat. A, Mental Class, and this type of classification meant that I was dangerous to my self and others. He then stated, I don't find any thing mentally wrong with you that needs treatment of any kind, we sometimes get a case like yours, someone gets angry at a prisoner and sends him here on a Psyc Jacket, and when he gets here we find nothing mentally wrong with him. However, he said, the rules is that I must keep you 30 days under observation in order to be positive of my finds. If I find no more than I have found now I will release you from here. Now don't worry about this report which is sent here, because it is our findings here that we go by, and not theirs. You won't be taking any medicine, you will just be on observations to confirm my findings. The doctor also promised me that he would see to it that I got my medicine which had been refused me, he said a doctor would call me out for it. This he did, he didn't have the sinner powder, but he did have a medicine that worked alright. After being there about ten days, a Dr. S. came by my cell and asked me how I felt, I told him I felt O.K. Then he asked me if I had lost any weight, I said, I don't know, it's been a long time since I have been on a scale but if I had lost any it wasn't very much because I don't notice any lost in weight. He then said, you look thin to me, I told him that was not unusual I have been skinney all my life, and so is my parents. He then said, if I give you some vitamine pills will you take them? Vitamins don't hurt anyone they are good for you I said, yes sir I'll take them, after about a half hour after Dr. S. was gone the M.T.A. brought me 4 pills, two I recognized as vitamins, and 2 was blood red with a black figure 8 on the side. I knew these wasn't vitamins, for I have worked in hospitals, they appeared to me to be some type of tranqualizers so I said to the M.T.A. those red pills isn't vitamins, the M.T.A. stated, this is what the doctor ordered, and you will have to take them. I asked him couldn't I refuse them, he said no, if you do, then I'll have some cons hold you and give you a shot, and that is much worst, so I said O.K. I'll take them, I put them in my mouth, and as I am 6 ft. 7 in. tall he couldn't see when I slipped them under my tongue. After he left I spit them out and took one of the red ones and bit it open, and rubbed it on my tongue, after a few minutes my tongue began to loose it's feelings, as I had suspected, they were tranqulizers. I had a cleanser box in my cell, so I hid the pills in the box so I could show them to my doctor when he came by, and ask him why was they bringing me tranqalizers when he had told me that I would be on no medication. The M.T.A. brought them three times daily, and after one week I had 42 of them, then custody came on a routine search of cells, they found the pills in the box, they asked me where did I get those pills, they then said these pills are dangerous, we are going to notify your doctor about this. After custody left, the M.T.A. came to my cell and took me out to his office, he was real nervous and scared, he said, why did you do that?, they have taken those pills to the Dr. panel to make some kind of excuse, I said, they made me sick. He then went in a smaller room and made a phone call, I could tell that he was calling Dr. S.'s home, because I heard him ask, is Dr. S. home, he then seemed to sense that I was listening so he spoke quieter and I couldn't hear anymore. After he finished talking to Dr. S. he went outside and came back with a big inmate, the inmate pulled a chair up beside me and sat down, then the M.T.A. said to me, I am going to fix you some medicine and you are going to drink it, or I will have this man hold you and give you a shot. Then the M.T.A. got a bottle of red liquid tranquilizers, and poured some medicine from 2 different bottles in the same cup as was the tranquilizer, he then told me to drink it, I knew that the red tranquilzer was given to mental patients a tea spoon full at a time, how he had poured me a two oz. cup full, plus medicine from two other bottles, I also knew that this was enough tranquilizer alone, let alone the other added medicine to dull, and slow the brain to the extent that there were strong possibilities of damaging the brain cells, so I said no I won't drink that, it's too much, and you know it is, then the convict caught my arm and put it behind me and said, are you going to drink it or not? Then I thought of something that I had learned while working in hospitals, that, the best thing to do when something has gotten in the stomach, and there is no available antidote for it, is to drink about a pint of water or more, then stick the finger in the throat forcing yourself to heave until all the water is out, repeat this until the water that comes back is crystal clear, after this, drink aprox. one pint of water so if any is left in the stomach, it will be deluted. Thinking of this, I says I'll drink it, and I did. Then I hurried back to my cell so I could heave it up, I could feel myself getting dizzy fast, when I got to my cell, I did what I had learned as I have described, after finishing, my throat, and tongue was burning badly from the medicine, it was very strong, it burned when I drank it, and also when coming back up. I sat down and began to wonder why were they so anxious to give me medicine when my doctor had told me that I needed none, and would be only on observations for 30 days, then I remembered what the officer at camp had said (they take up where we leave off at), then I concentrated on how the medicine was working on me, although I did not give the full dose a chance to pass to my blood some of it had, due to the time that elapsed, coming from the M.T.A. Office back to my cell, I felt dizzy. Some dullness, and a weakness seemed to cover my whole body. This led me to believe that if I had kept the full dose in me, permitting it to pass to my blood, I would have been in a terrible state, and impossible to have clear thinking, and rendering me to a state of helplessness, and stupidity. I also did not believe that my doctor knew this was going on, for he seemed to be an honest, and just man, and a man who one could trust. This opinion proved to be true later. Having the trust that I did have in my doctor, led me to also suspect that this Dr. S., and the M.T.A. were institution crooks, and was purposely trying to Psyc me out, probably in order to support the phony Psyc charge which I received at C.C.C. The judge had promised me while in his court, that he (the judge) would prepare me a writ of habeas corpus, and forward it to me, so I could follow my case up to fight the phony Psyc charge, the judge had sent it, and I know Dr. S., and the M.T.A. was aware of it because they censor our mail, it was also possible that someone at C.C.C. had made contact with them. Some of my calculations I found to be true, for Dr. S. called me out the next day and told me that the Panel was going to call me that day about those pills, he then told me that I should tell the doctor Pannel that I wanted to take those pills, because they were good for me, and many people take them to improve their health, he did not know that I had learned alot about medicines while working in hospitals. I could see that this Dr. (S.) was trying to cover up something, and that he was a crooked doctor, I figured it unwise to tell him that I wouldn't do this which he was advising me to do, so to play it safe, I said allright I would tell the Panel this, he (Dr. S.) assured me that this was the thing to do, and that he was trying to help me. The doctor Pannel called me in to see them around noon, when I entered their room I saw my doctor and several more doctors sitting in the room, I found that just as I had guessed, my doctor knew nothing about these pills being given to me, the other doctors also looked very surprised, and they seemed to sense that something out of ordernarily was going on in the hospital. They began asking, who gave me those pills, and if I had taken any of them, my doctor told me, if you took any of these pills tell me, and how many you took, because it is very important for us to know, I started at the beginning and told him everything, after I finished, one of the doctors asked the others, did anyone tell Doctor S. to do this? They all said no they had not. My doctor said to me, this won't happen again so don't worry about this happening again we will see to it that it doesn't. I did the rest of my observation time, and as my doctor promised, I was released to General Population to serve my sentence.

After several months I was transfered to a Minimum Camp, at C.M.C. West. Upon arrival, my medicine was immediately taken, I was given castor-oil and sometimes milk of magnesia, strong laxatives was all I was able to obtain from Dr. M. After several months I grew so weak from taking laxatives, and lost around 40 pounds, I felt that I couldn't last much longer, so I went to the Administration and asked for a transfer to the East Side, which is only about two blocks away, I was advised by the older inmates there at the camp, the staff could not force anyone to stay there, and that it was my rights to refuse to stay at any camp, they further advised me, that I looked very bad, and that if I didn't find a way to get off laxatives, I looked as I might soon die. A few days later, I took one of the longest heaving spells from taking laxatives that I had ever encountered. I had had spells like this before from laxatives, but never this long, my stomach had grown too weak to hold food, or liquids, so I went to custody's office and told them that I refuse to stay any further at camp, and I wish to be sent some place where I can get my proper medicine so I won't have to take laxatives, because they are making me unbearably sick. They tried to talk me into staying on, but I said no I have made up my mind. Then they got rough, one Lt. told me, why don't you just walk off, theres nothing to hold you, I said no, I don't wish to do any thing against the rules, the Lt. said, why not? I got a new gun I bought and I am just raring to try it out, then the Lt., threatened to put knots on my head, I knew what these threats was for, the older inmates had warned me that if they could not talk me into staying, then they would try to make me get a violation, by provoking me into cursing them, or trying to fight them, I was told by the inmates, that the staff here don't like for inmates to transfer by request, they say it makes the place look bad, they have the public thinking that this place is nice, when It's really hell. We just as soon as not have a doctor here for what benefit Dr. M. is, men have went to him for as little as a laxative when they hadn't had a bowel movement in eight, or ten days. M. would refuse them any, and would tell them to drink 20 glasses of water, then sit on the toilet and wait, this might not sound true, but old men have died here from a small problem as constipation. And feller if you have bowl troubles, you had better leave here, even if you have to walk off, don't let them provoke you into getting a charge, they will have to remove you. So I knew what they were doing, so I stayed humble, and mannerable. After they couldn't provoke me, the Lt., then asked me do you remember that Psyc jacket they have on you boy, I said, Yesser I do, and it was a phoney, I was released in Vacaville Medical Center, after 30 days observation, with no medical treatment while there. The Lt. then said, this isn't Vacaville, now make your mind up boy what you will have, back to your dorm, or off to the head shrinker. This sounded very bad for me, and I feared that the next Psyc doctor might not be as fair as my doctor at Vacaville was, I thought about what the older inmates had said, stick with it, don't give up, the Lt. asked, well what will it be boy, it's all up to you. I said, I won't stay, I need my bowl medicine very bad and I can't get any here, so I have no other choice. The Lt. then told the other officers, dump him on the Psyc. Doctor at the East Side. They then took me across to the East Side, and locked me in the Psyc Ward, this was on a Friday, and the doctor wasn't in until Monday. The M.T.A., there started bringing me pills right away before I had even seen a doctor, I accepted the pills, for I did not want any confusion before I could see the doctor. I would put the pills in my mouth, and when the M.T.A. would leave I would spit them in the camode and flush them. When Dr. B. (the Psyc Dr.) came in that Monday, he talked with me, and asked, what happened at the West Side, I told Dr. B., my reasons for wanting to leave the West Side, and all that occured while leaving, Dr. B. then said, they says here in the report, that you haven't been taking your medicine, I asked, is they refering to Psyc medicine? He said yes, I said, I am not on any Psyc medicine and have never in my life been on any, if you will look in my medical files, you will find that I was never on any medicine, I was held under 30 days observation, and released. Dr. B. said, I have saw your file already, and I was confused of what they are talking about, I said ask the Dr. over there, he will tell you that I don't take any Psyc medicine, Dr. B. said the Dr. there is the one who made the report, have you been in any trouble prior to now there? I said none what so ever, Dr. B. then said, let me check your disaplinary file and see if I can make some kind of sense here, he checked my file, and when he had finished, he (Dr. B.) said, I can't find nothing that you have done, silly people, usually does silly things, but I don't find anything you did, and the excuse that you have given me for wanting to leave there sounds logical enough. Then Dr. B. said, you have been dropped on me is what I am thinking, and now it is up to me to do something with you, now what do you want to do? Do you want to transfer some place you have in mind, or do you think you would like to do your time here? I said, I don't have anyplace in mind because I don't know any of the places, although I have been in Calif. 30 years I have never been to Calif. Prison before, so I don't know anyplace to say I would like, I just want to be someplace where I can get my proper medication for my bowls, I will just as soon stay here if I can get proper medicine. The doctor then said, we have a large pharmacy here, I don't think you will have any trouble getting it here, I'll send you to the M.D. as soon as possible. Now you are still registered as living at the West

Side, so I will have to keep you here in the hospital until I can get you a transfer O.K? Have you ever worked in a hospital before? I said that I had, then told him of some hospitals I had worked, and what I did there, he said well that's good, we can use you, how about working until your transfer comes back? I will have to send it to Sacramento, that will take about three weeks, when it does come back I'll move you to A quad in General Population.

I worked there in the hospital until the transfer came back, then I was moved to A quad living quarters, the next day I was assigned to a hospital attendant job, at D. Quad, doctor B. had told me, that when I was assigned to permanet quarters, I was to go see Doctor W., the M.D., and get my bowl medicine. I went to Dr. W. to get it, when I met him I found that the West Side had already talked to him about me, and whatever they had told him, had him in a very angry mood, I tried to explain to him that, I had suffered 13 years with bowl troubles, and that I had been operated on for it, and the medicine which I have taken 13 years for my bowls, I was refused it at the West Side. He constantly accused me of walking out on the West-Side for no good reason at all, and told me that I should have stayed there, and that Dr. M., was perfectly capable of carring for me. Eventually, he had me lay on a table, he pressed me in the stomach several times, when he had finished, he said, I find nothing wrong with your stomach, and I am not giving you any medicine, you will get a notice to come in for exrays, I asked, how long will that be doctor? he says, we will send you a notice. I went to Doctor B., and told him that Dr. W., had not issued me any medicine, and that I needed it very badly. Dr. B. tole me, over where you are working, you see the M.T.A., and tell him the medicine you need, he might have it there, I will call him and tell him it is alright to let you have it if he has it, I went to where I worked and told the M.T.A. what the Dr. said. The M.T.A. said, Yes, the Dr. just called, but the medicine I think you want, I don't have I only have laxatives, I told him that I would have to take that, so he gave me a container with milk-of-magnesia, and a bottle of castor oil. I constantly had heaving spells, and stayed sick all the time, I knew this was from taking too many laxatives, but if I didn't take the laxatives, then I would suffer with my bowl troubles, I guessed the bowl troubles to be more dangerous than the laxatives for when my bowls started troubling me, it don't reach a certain stage and stop, it gets worst as time goes by, and never ceases to get worst until I take my medicine it starts by making me sick at the stomach. If I allow enough time to elapse before taking medicine, my stomach begans cramping to the extent that it doubles me over, at that point I am heaving, cramping, and having flutters. Even though laxatives make me sick, they have never had me in the shape that my bowl sickness has had me in. I was called in to take the exray, which Dr. W. had mentioned after Dr. W. say the exray, he said, I don't see anything on the exray wrong with your stomach, and I will not give you any medicine unless I can see something I said, whatever is causing my stomach troubles don't show on exray. My doctors outside couldn't find it on exray, they were still in the process of trying to find what was causing my stomach troubles when I was jailed, that's why they cut on my herneries in Tucson, Ariz., the doctors were suspecting that the hernies were causing the troubles. Dr. W. then said, well I am not giving you any medicine, so don't come back in here for any because the answer will still be no. At this time, my appearance to the Adult Authority Board for parole was about 6 months away, I figured if I could find some way to obtain some medicine, and get off laxitives, I possibly could make it to the Board for parole, then I would be free to get my own medicine, so I began to contact inmates who worked the closest to medication inside the regular building where the pharmacy is. I finally made contact with the best inmate for this purpose. I had forgotten the name of the pills that I wanted, and had used when out of Prison for my ailment, so I had to describe them to him, I told him they were about the size of a jelly bean, and cherry red color, and they could be squeezed between the fingers like a piece of rubber, they are used for the purpose of abstracting water from the blood, that dumps into the bowl, causing a normal bowl movement, and keeping the stage soft at all times. The inmate said, I am pretty sure I have seen those pills, I think I know the ones you are talking about. A few days later he brought me a small box of pills, they were the right ones. I started taking them, and about a week later I had stopped heaving, and feeling sick at my stomach, at that time, I had lost weight down to 150 lbs., I had lost 60 lbs. while in prison, about one month later I had gained up to 175 lbs., and my stomach was feeling almost perfect, only sometimes I would be sick at my stomach, and never seriously like before. I continued to work as hospital attendant in D. Quad, and three months before my board appearance the inmate counsiler, Mr. H., called me to his office, he said, you are going to the board soon, I have looked in your file, and I see where you got smart with the people at C.C.C. in 1968. I know Mr. T., and several of the officials there have been friends of mine for a long time. They are very nice people, you must have been wrong to have it with them, so don't expect any help from me. I said, I was forced to take those people to court about my medicine which they had refused me, and by doing so, it resulted into the incident. I had no other choice but to go to court, and I wasn't trying to be smart. He wouldn't accept any part of my explanation as being legitement, he says to me, as far as I am concerned, you are one of those smart ellicks, and if you come here and get smart with these officials, you are really going to be in trouble. I am telling you now, when you go to that board, I personally am going to see that you do 5 years, if not the whole 14 years. I said do you mean I have to do that much time on a thirty six dollar check? Mr. H. said, we have smart bastards here doing more time than that, for less, I said, going to court is not being smart, or in violation of any laws. Mr. H., then said, we call the shots around here, and not you, and nigger, don't you froget that. I knew then that the man was extremely prejuidice, and that I did not have a fair chance with a man of this type, so I turned and walked out. The next time I saw Mr. H., was around three weeks later. I had taken on extra work besides my regular hospital job, I would go to the mess hall at noon, and help serve noon meals, which consisted of about 45 minutes, I did this in order to get extra foods, and extra meat, this particular day, I had gone to the mess hall, and worked my approximately 45 minutes and returned to my job at the hospital as it was understood by my boss at the hospital, and the boss at the mess hall for me to do. During sometime after I left the mess hall after serving noon meal, the fellows that work regular in the mess hall became in a dispute over their jobs, and they all walked off the job. When Mr. H. heard about it, by him seeing me serve lunch in the mess hall, he thought I worked regular there, so he called me to his office, and asked, why did you niggers walk out of that kitchen? I turned without saying a word and walked out of his office. He came to the door and said, wait till you meet the board, do you think you are going to make it? A few days before board time, my boss at the hospital, Mr. A., made out my work report for the board, an above average one, and told me, Fartheree I hope you make it, You are a good worker, and you have in 18 months, I see no reason why you shouldn't make it, so good luck, Dr. B., had also told me prior to this, that he also thought I was a good worker, and that I had did a good job at the hospital, he said, I will turn in your report to the board as a good one. You have caused no trouble since you have been here, and I see no reason why they should not pass you at the board. When the parole board came, on the same day that Dr. B. was to make his panel report on me, which states the type of criminal a man is, and weighs heavy with the boards decision on a person's making parole, Dr. B. transfered to another institution, this left an assistant, Dr. K., to make the report that Dr. B. would have made. Mr. H., (the inmates counsler), went to Dr. K., and persuaded Dr. K. into letting him (Mr. H.) make out the doctors report, by doing this, it enabled Mr. H. to make the doctors report identical with his (Mr. H.'s) counselors report, which also goes to the board. By the doctors report being the most powerfull report that can be produced to the board, and the most considered, and comparing with the counselors report, is enough alone to make one miss parole. Regardless of how many other good reports, this combination which Mr. H. had succeeded in preparing for the board would over power them all. At this time I had a recommendation filed for the purpose of the board, by the Calif. Dept. of Public Health, stating, that I was to be commended for volunteering as a subject in a research study by the unniversity of Calif. School of Dentistry, and the Calif. Dept. of Public Health. He (Alonzo Fartheree) received no compensation for his cooperation this was signed by, Dr. C., C.M.C. East Facility. I had an above average work report from my boss, signed by mr. A. I had had no displenary at C.M.C. East, I had in 18 months on a thirty six dollar check charge, and a job waiting for me. When I was called to appear to the board, Mr. H. was there. I was asked a few questions by the board members, and turned down for the setting of my time. After the Board appearance, I wrote the head man of the Adult Authority telling him what Mr. H. had did, I asked Mr. T. (head man of A.A.) to investigate my aleged accusations against Mr. H., and grant me a reappearance to the board, so that I may have a fair and equal chance, of obtaining my time being set. Mr. T. never did answer my letter. I then wrote the board, they (the board) likewise, never did answer. I realized then that my best interest in order to obtain a fair chance at parole the next year, was to try and change counselors, to get away from Mr. H. I went to Mr. H., as the rules in prison requires us, to first see our appointed counselor in anything we are attempting to do. I asked Mr. H. about a change, he flat refused me, I could tell this was very important, that I did get from under him as my counselor, for I would never have a chance at parole as long as I was under him, so as I went to higher security officials and explained my case to them, I did suceed in getting transfered to a Mr. R., an inmate counselor at A. Quad. I also quit my job at the hospital, and took a job at the shoe factory, in order to be as far away from Mr. H. as possible. After about three weeks of doing fine on my job, and living quarters, I came from work one day, and there on my door, I had a notice to move back to Mr. H.'s quarters. This automatically gives him jurisdiction over me, I went to the Quad Sargent and asked him, why am I being moved back to Mr. H., what have I done? He (Sargent S.) said, I don't know why you are being moved back, I found out that Sargent S. did know why, an inmate who works in Sargent S.'s office told me that Mr. H. had come to Sargent S. office a few days prior to this and asked him to sign a request pertaining to me being moved back to his (Mr. H.) counseling area. When I was moved back, I went to Mr. H., and told him that I was very disappointed, and I did not want to be under him anymore because I felt that he would not give me a fair, and equal chance at parole, I also told him, that it was my opinion that his unfairness, and hate for me, stimmed from extremely prejudice he had for Black People. He said, yes, I am prejudice to niggers, why shouldn't I be? Do you read the papers? Do you look at the T.V.? If you were a white man, and I was a nigger, wouldn't you be prejudice of me? I'll answer that question for you, yes you would be, the way you niggers is caring out, you need more than being prejudice to you. I then walked out. I then went to the security Lt. Mr. K., I told him all that had happened, and how I felt about Mr. H., I then Asked Mr. K., would he transfer me to Chino close to my relatives, so they could have a chance to visit me. I had been so far away, they had only visited me once since being in prison, and Chino will be close enough for them to visit me regular and also get me away from Mr. H. Mr. K. said, this will have to be started with your counselor, so go tell Mr. H. that you had a talk with me, and I said it's o.k. by me if he will put you up for transfer to Chino, we have no objections of you transfering. I went to Mr. H. and told him what Mr. K. had said, Mr. H. was very angry, he said, I will not put you up for a transfer for Chino, and you are going to learn that around here you don't run nothing, you do as you are told. I said, I know I can't run nothing here, I am only asking, Mr. H. then said, get out of my office, so I went back to Mr. K. and told him what Mr. H. said. Mr. K. then prepared a memo, and told me to take it to Mr. S., this was Mr. H.'s boss, I carried the memo to Mr. S., he read it, then

asked me to fill out a request for Chino, I did, then S. said, H.'s
security wants this man placed on docket, to appear before the
committee for transfer to Chino. When my request did reach the
Roverboard [Board which decides transfers] Mr. H. had changed
my request to Chino, into a request to Folsom. This is the
worst prison in the state of Calif., and is for dangerous, and
violant prisoners, usually when a man is sent to Folsom, he has
attacked officers, or killed other prisoners. I had not been in one
fight since I had been confined, my disaplinary record in prison
was a good one. When the roverboard received my request, and
thinking that I had requested Folsom, it was O.kayed. I learned
too late to try to have it stopped. I went to the priest to see if he
could do anything, the priest called Mr. H., and asked him, why is
Fartheree being sent to Folsom? He has caused us no trouble at
all here, Mr. H. told the priest That he (Mr. H.) did not know
why I was being sent to Folsom, the priest called several security
officials, but no one seemed to know what caused me to being
sent to Folsom. The priest said, you have nothing in your displinary record that justified you going to Folsom, but keep your
chin up, and go ahead, maybe they will transfer you when you
get there, and it might still work out alright. So I was sent off to
Folsom.

Upon my arrival at Folsom, I ran into trouble about my medicine, the doctors didn't have what I needed, and didn't seem to
have time to listen to my pleas, so I went to Warden Gunn, and
explained the whole thing to him, and told him that I didn't want
to worry anyone, but I had to have my medicine, or I would come
down with serious troubles with my stomach, and bowls. Mr.
Gunn said, I'll have an officer to escort you to the Chief Medical
Doctor, you explain it to him as you did to me, he should help
you. The officer carried me to the Chief M.D. Mr. R., I told
the doctor my troubles, explaining that I must have my medicine
to avoid troubles. Dr. R. said, we don't have that kind of medicine here. I asked him would he permit me to buy it he said no,
no such thing here. He gave me a prescription for some laxative
pills, and left the room. These pills seemed very old, and weak,

after taking them several days I began to heave, I knew then that the pills was not working. I thought if I could get them to give me some mineral oil to go along with the pills, they might work well enough to get by on, so I went to the hospital to try, I had to wait in a long line, so while waiting, I noticed that there were three doctors, Dr. R., Dr. Y., and Dr. K. I noticed that Dr. Y. was awful mean to the prisoners, and Dr. R., was almost identical, but, Dr. K. I noticed was very kind to the patients, so I decided to see Dr. K., when I was called. When I was called, I was motioned over to Dr. Y., the meanest one, so I said, doctor I came to see the doctor that is over there please, Dr. Y. didn't say yes, nor did he say no, he just stepped to the door and called an officer and said, throw this man out, the officer led me outside, I asked the officer, why did he do that? The officer said, I don't know, what did you do in there? I said nothing, I just asked him could I see the other doctor, the officer said, well that's why, he don't allow you to ask for certain doctors.

I have never been able to obtain my proper medicine since I have been here, only laxatives that is leaving me weak, and loosing weight all the time. On or about the month of August I was given a job working in the cannery, I had to walk five storys of stairs six times daily, this pulled my operation, causing it to swell, and infect, deep inside, and on, or about, the last of Sept., 1970, Dr. R., the Chief Medical Doctor, did make and incesion on my left side in the same place which I was cut on before, and let out puss, to try to control the swelling and pain. He tried to pull some stitches out, which he said was still in my side, he could not pull them, so Dr. R. said, it's some stitches in there, but I don't want to cut you any deeper because I am not prepared for that then he gave me a three day lay in, and gave me a slip to have my side dressed every 24 hours, when my 3 day layin was up, my wound had infected, due to the fact that it wasn't being dressed often enough, once every 24 hours wasn't keeping it clean so it had infected, very badly. I went to Dr. R., and said doctor I would like to get a further layin, my wound has infected very badly, and also I need to get this dressed more often than once every 24 hours, Dr. R. said, you can work alright, and once a day is enought to dress that wound. I then went to our prison chaplin, and showed my wound to him, and asked him wasn't it something he could do to help me obtain a layin for I wasn't in shape to work, the chaplin said, that is a bad looking place alright, but there is nothing I can do, I am sorry, I do think you need to be in bed with a wound like that. Seeing the terrible shape it was in the chaplin asked, is that blood coming out of there? I said, it's blood, and puss. The Chaplin then said, I am very sorry I can't help you, try some of the officials, maybe they will help you, so I went to my prison counselor, he told me the same thing, that it was out of his power to help me. So I went on to work. After several days my boss at the cannery grew uneasy about me, he had seen my wound, and had seen me try to clean it several times on the job he asked me, won't the doctor give you a layin with a wound like that? I said, no sir, the Dr. refused me. My boss then said, we have no power over the doctors division, but we do have power to lay you off from here, this he did. I was then assigned to a tier tindering job, in 3 Bldg, I still continued to infect worse, as time went by. I probably would have blood poison, if it had not been for another inmate, he had noticed the condition I was in, and told me that I had better do something or I might be blood poisoned. He had a friend that worked in the hospital, so he had his friend to steel cotton, and medication, and bring it to me. I started cleaning, and dressing my wound 4 or 5 times daily, it stopped the infection and brought the swelling down. The only time I swell now, is when I walk too much, my sack hangs heavy, and causes my operation to swell, because I have no Jockey strap now to hold my sock up. My doctor outside gave me one to wear, I have a permit to show that it is necessary I use a jocky strap, my jocky strap rotted out, and tore up, I went to Dr. R., and showed him my permit, and asked him would he issue me a order for one, he turned me down, although the prison pharmacy has plenty of them. At this writing of this writt, my side is swollen, and I constantly have severe stomach and bowl attacks. My operation that I had in 1968, has

never healed completely, my medical problems is worsening all
the time.

In November 1970, I went back for consideration of parole.
I had in 2 and one half years on a thirty six dollar check (forgery),
my displinary record in prison showed that I had 5 days confinement, in the two and one half years that I had been in prison,
two days confinement in 1968, due to me not being able to
work, this was at Ceirra-conservation-Center, and three days confinement at Folsom 1970, due to a report, stating, that I was
late from chow. The board officials consisted of two men, a
Mr. ————, and Mr. ———— and my counselor Mr. R., the
board officials had a letter from Mr. J. stating that, If I was released I had a job awaiting me at the San Diego Ship Builders,
and it was signed by the Superintendent of the shipyard. I could
tell that these two board officials had come with no intentions of
letting me go. I had a good prison record they wasn't able to
obtain a legal excuse to turn me down, so they went to my past
record, back as far as 1950, and in 1957, and some fights that
I have had in my days coming up. They even went to a charge
that I had been found not guilty of, these things they had to use
to claim an excuse to turn me down, my counselor argued that
they were being *unfare* with me, and that I had served enough
time for the crime I did. They would not listen to him, they
turned me down. I could tell that they had pressure behind them,
and no please, or good showings would make them do different,
than turn me down. I do believe that there is certain officials
that is working in the California Prison System, that know the
wrong that they have done me, stimming from 1968, up until now,
and is having me held in prison, in fear of my release being an
exposure to their wicked way of doing in prison. I also feel that
my only way of getting a fair, and equal chance of being released
from prison is through the court.

After the board meeting was over, I knew then that I will never
walk out of prison alive. I could see that the authority was working
in cahoots with my being held in prison, they know that I am
infected badly in my stomach, and have been for months. I don't

see how cancer hasn't already set in due to the lengthy time that I have been infected. I know that I will die soon if I don't get help real soon, so I wrote a writ, and in it I filed damages on eleven officials of the Calif. Dept. of Corrections for the sum of sixteen and ½ million dollars, all total I complained and charged them with, long suffering for the period of two years, and eight months, from cruel, unusual and inhumane punishment, that has been, and is now being done upon me, by the defendants, and accused them of violating the guaranteed Federal Protected Laws of the Constitution of the United States of America; Under the 8th and 14th amendments, and of the Calif. Constitutional Laws, that guarantees against such acts, under art. 1, Sec. 13, and these provisions guaranteed by art. 1, Sec. 22; art. 1, Sec. 23. I filed my complaint in the United States District Court of the Eastern District of Calif. on Jan. 28th 1971. I received notice from the court that my complaint was accepted, and filed civil no. S1945, in Judge Thomas J. McBride's Court. A few days later I received word from the Marshal that he was ready to serve summons, and to send the proper copies of the complaint, and summons copies this I did do, then on Feb. 2nd, five days later I was placed in confinement and told by the officials that this was being done because someone was trying to hurt me, this is as phony as an excuse can get. I have been in prison two years, and 8 months, and haven't ever had one fight, the officials did this in order to halt further actions in my suit. I am placed in a confinement away from typewriter, or any other legal material, or law books that I need badly to continue prosecuting of my case. They are atempting to stop all my action, and in time, if they succeed my case would be thrown out of court for failing to prosecute, they are also punishing me, all medication for cleaning and bandaging my badly infected wound has been taken away from me, I wash the puss and corrupt blood from my wound, and then pack it with toilet paper, this is germy I know, but I have asked many times for medication, and cotton, but they refused me each time so toilet paper is all I have and clear water. I hurt so bad at night, but I have nothing to ease the pain. I will soon die I know, if help don't come soon, and all because I took them to court in 1968. I did no wrong, but the people that run these institutions are clan style people, and well organized and by me taking them to court in 1968, and this time, I am branded by them as they call it, (a smart convict). And for no other reason, by their hands I have to slowly die, I am in for a 36 dollar check, and have served at this time 2 years and 8 months.

ALONZO A. FARTHEREE

Oct. 1970
San Quentin

Dear Sir:

I was enroute to the gymnasium located in San Quentin's lower yard for the purpose of conducting inmate Advisory Council Quarterly Film Bookings with Coach T. L. Baker, when I happen to observe two correctional officers approaching a table where inmate Brooks (whom I knew) was in the process of studying strategy moves in an independent game of chess. Within a few seconds all three were moving off in the direction of the upper yard. Some approximate 3 hours following, it was related to me that some inmate by the name of Brooks had been placed in a "quiet cell" in "B" Section of the South Block and severely beaten; then deposited into a cell on the psychiatric ward pending an immediate transfer to Vacaville.

In May of 1970, (some 16 months after the Brooks occurrence) I was accused of violating institutional rule D-2401, "circumventing the mail" and as a result was lodged into the isolation section of the Adjustment Center. It was here that I discovered inmate Brooks having been returned to San Quentin after enduring many months of total isolation from the inmate population at Vacaville. Because of the extent of his injury as suffered from his beating as well as being unable to maneuver himself upon the isolation cell's iron bunk, his mattress had been placed on the cement floor which served as his bed, library, meal table, correspondence and legal desk. Occasionally, one man at a time was allowed 10 minutes exercise periods directly outside the cell area, and as a result of this, I often heard inmate Brooks pleading for crutches in order to attempt to take advantage of this privilege. This request as well as dental, legal material and return to the normal living conditions of prison life were continuously denied. The latter was based upon his incapacitation. Once a week we were permitted to use the shower facility at the far end of the tank and during my confinement in the Adjustment Center, subject was required by prison guards to drag himself in his underwear to and from this area. This scene was so distressing to me, that I made it a point to inquire one day of Sergeant S. if it would be permissible for me to carry this man to and from the shower, to which, the response was for me to mind my own business. Naturally, it was impossible for me to acquire any other impression except that there seems to be in existence an undertaking to dehumanize or vegetate inmate Brooks. I can only relate that I have always found this man to be a very sagacious person, well versed in matters of law and certainly far from being a psychiatric problem.

Austin Wells

Ralph Chacon, whose letters follow, is serving several life sentences concurrently. He was recently transferred from the hole at Soledad (O Wing) to the California Medical Facility at Vacaville.

Soledad
June 16, 1970

Dear Mrs. Fay Stender,

For five years I have not seen the sun, one and a half on death row and the rest in the hole. Where guards beat on guys for almost nothing, where one Doctor H. took convicts by force out of their cells and gave them shock treatments strapped on a common barber shop chair. Where I am now at in the hole from July 1967 til March 16, 1970. I had a clear record but I was to remain in the hole, O-Wing where again I been set up and shot at beaten and all because I was to keep in the hole. I been in seven prisons since my eighteenth birthday, I'm twenty seven now, I committed crimes but always was force to plead guilty because I feared what waited if I didn't—a beating by guards. They don't put me in a hospital, because they rather gas me, at San Quentin. There's more but this is just a little about O-Wing and me.

Ralph M. Chacon

June 1970
Soledad

Dear Fay Stender,

You got my permission to publish anything I write, because
everything I write is true. And I'll die or give my life if I am
proven wrong. I want you to know Mrs. Stender that I'm not concern with my life if I got to live it behind bars, not with the
corruption I've seen and been put through purposely. Only if
I can be set free, can I ever get peace of mind, or rather be put
to death. Not after what these people, "the prison staff" has
made of me.

Prison personnel gets weak inmates, to testify falsely when
something happens that they can't see themselves, and on innocent people. They even get their own guards to testify falsely
and even when they see it themselves. And it works sometimes,
and when it doesn't, that person won't see the streets for a long
time, and sometimes they set them up to get killed. Who would
take the word of a prisoner against the word of a suppose to be
respectable guard and false witness included. They don't care
about any prisoner as long as someone pays. I've died so many
times already mentally that I guess once more wouldn't hurt.
I probably wouldn't even feel it. I am not an animal, just someone
that needs help or they will kill me. I need help tell someone to
help me, you can surely do that for a good human being thats done
wrong purposely. I want to live and let live, but its hard in prison
for a loner whose life is in a strange world, lost and with nothing
but death following me. I know the guards are trying to set me up
now, to get killed, but like I said I died so many times I guess one
more isn't going to hurt. My trial starts July 1st. My own attorney, Doctor H. said I was competent. And I don't even know
any thing about court or law. But I can fight lies with the truth.
Anyway I been set up five or six times with people hostile to me.
Twice I let my anger guide me, one has resulted in a death the
other with 50 or 60 stab wounds. The other times I have held
back because of a promise to my mother, and even that I broke,

because misunderstanding was going on caused by the guards. I wish Mrs. Stender that I have never come out of Death Row, cause I've gone through a worse hell here in O-Wing. I wish you luck and best wishes.

Truly Yours,
Ralph M. Chacon

California Medical
Facility
Feb. 7, 1971

Dear Fay Stender:

I finally got to see you, and know how wonderful you really are, and as always—beautiful.

I didn't have much to say because I was really surprised. I guess I was still kind of sleepy. The medication I get keeps me drowsy all day, and when I receive visits, I feel like I'm in a quiet trance unable to communicate with whom I'm speaking to but today afterwards my whole day became brighter. So thank you many many times Mrs. Stender I really enjoyed talking with you. And now I close wishing you the very best, also to your family.

Respectfully
Ralph Chacon

Vacaville
April, 1971

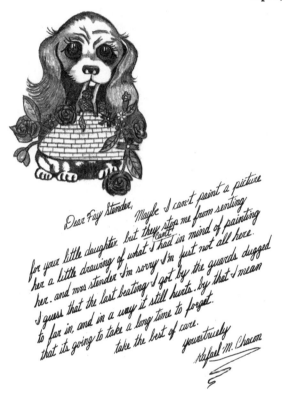

Dear Fay Stender,
Maybe I can't paint a picture for your little daughter. but they stop me from senting her a little drawing of what I had in mind of painting her. and mrs stender I'm sorry I'm just not all here. I guess that the last beating I got by the guards dugged to far in. and in a way it still hurts. by that I mean that its going to take a long time to forget.
take the best of care.
yourstruely
Rafael M. Chacon

Soledad
Jan 5, 1971

[*From Mass of Desperate Papers*]

As a human being I have grown dependent on belonging to others and as a creature I am dependent upon freedom and exposure to nature—as a prisoner I am removed from both of these things.

I am so afraid that my mind cannot accept reality of being

trapped here. On approaching realization—big hysterical claustrophobia—suffocation comes. I realize that I live in delusion of hope of possible release or resumption of life. Life is ended. I can no longer live in imagination of hope. My mind is broken— but I cannot admit that this is true. Many here go insane too . . . They scream in terror as articulated patterns of mind terminate abandoning them to the reality they can no longer avoid. One screamed "Hot and cold, hot and cold," Another "Help me, please let me out of here." I know this fear now and often. To realize that I am subject to people who regard me in such a way as to treat me thus is fear but real terror is the phenomena itself —the moments passing. This is attack on mind—to torture. It makes no sense to express reasons why I should not be tortured this way because there is no sane reason to do this to me. These words are the only thing my mind hangs on as I write I am unable to re-read. Please do what you can to get me out of here as soon as possible. Yes, I am weak. Yes, I am insane. Reality is claustrophobia for me now. Hysteria.

It is Sunday morning, about 3 a.m. Rolling and smoking cigarettes blot out fear—divert. That everyone has abandoned me to this leaves no identity—no love—no together with any-one. To be alone, on an island, would be different. This is like a mine cave in where nobody digs to free you.

Smoke smoke. Nobody responds to what I say. But this is song for life and is good-right song and laws song-to assassinate is bad-wrong song. So I say I cannot communicate with anybody. I write many letters mail none for a long time. Then hysteria allayed by writing letter and temporarily put down by sending but only gone by release. Then not gone until law made right, follow outside too. I am afraid of law, I do not respect it. This is what has bothered my whole life—I do not trust law for good reason. I am afraid of people for good reason. Truth and right and equality no good against guns, or money, or force.

Bryce

San Quentin
March 18th, 1971

Dear Brothers & Sisters,

At 11:15 A.M. on March 15th, 1971 I arrived at San Quentin State Prison. The journey from Folsom took some five and a half hours on board the CDC Bus. Upon entering the Sally Port Gate I found myself waiting another hour and a half to be changed from my traveling whites to a pair of blue coveralls. About 1:30 an officer called my name and took me to the captains office where I cooled my heels for another 20 minutes, and at that point without a word being said, I was escorted to isolation in "B" Section, with a stop off at the prison hospital for a physical. The physical consisted of an MTA saying: "Is there any physical reason why you can't go to isolation? I looked at the two officers who were escorting me, and thought that my health could turn pretty bad if I said anything but what they wanted to hear. As far as I know, nothing short of death will keep you out of the hole, I didn't feel like arguing. I answered "No," and to "B" Section I went. At Folsom, I didn't even go to the hospital for a physical before going to the hole on past occasions, so I was at least that far ahead, if being 15 feet away from an M.T.A., fully clothed and answering a single "No" is very far ahead! Once in "B" Section, I was told to strip, open my mouth, raise my arms, lift my balls, turn around, bend over, spread my cheeks, lift my feet (one at a time) and redress. Meanwhile the pigs searched my coveralls, shorts, socks, and shoes. I was then given two, not too clean blankets and escorted to cell number 30 on the first floor. The cell measures, I would estimate, four and a half feet wide, seven and a half feet floor to celling, and say ten feet deep. The front of the cell is barred with 13 bars, seven making up the door and six the rest of the front. In the center of six is a tray slot three inches high and 14 inches wide. The door is fitted with a heavy lock and above the door is a bar which is let down giving extra security. As I entered the cell I smelled the odor of rotting matter, and discovered a pile of trash in the back corner of the cell. The floor was filthy with dirt clay thick. On the left was a wall bunk with an even dirtier cotton pad. One end of the pad is mildewed, a dark gray mold covering it. In the center of the pad is a big cigar burn and the rest of the pad is water marked and gray with dirt. The bunk, I soon discovered, cannot be slept on, that is if one wishes to walk in the morning. The springs have been bent all out of shape by some previous occupant who I'd say jumped up and down on the springs themselves, leaving two depressions about two feet in diameter and six to eight inches deep, into which the cotton pad sinks. Overhead, the ceiling has a single 60 watt light bulb in an exposed light socket. There is no light switch, but you find you can screw the bulb in and out to turn it on and off. On the back wall is a toilet bowl and a sink, both which need a cleaning. You have no towel, no toilet paper and nothing but your hands to drink water out of. The first job involved throwing out whatever was loose, or would come loose from the floor. A convict was on the floor outside of the cell, and I inquired of him about getting some cell supplies so I could set up house keeping. He said "yah" and moved on. The tier tender passed by several more times and I asked him again and got the same answer. He had a cup of coffee in his hand and he was always on the heel and toe. About five o'clock I got my first meal at San Quentin, having missed lunch, only to find I didn't have anything to eat it with. The tray sat in the tray slot and I just looked at it, and seeing the tier tender I asked him what I was going to use to eat it with. Ten minutes later he brought me a plastic spoon which obviously had been used by someone else, for it still had traces of food on it. After washing it in cold water, I sat down to a cold meal of lamb stew, of which I could only down about one spoonful. I put the tray back in the tray slot and about five minutes later the tier tender returned carrying a coffee pot. I had no cup, so I didn't get any coffee which was alright with me, because I gave coffee up four years ago. But I did need a cup, and he said he'd get me one. That night I placed the mattress on the floor, covered it with one of the two blankets I had, and using my T-Shirt for a pillow, kicked off my shoes and pulled the second blanket over me. Breakfast was served at about 5:30 A.M., and I still didn't have a cup. I also needed a tooth brush, toilet paper and most important a pencil. On Tuesday, I scored a cup, towel and a shower with clean underwear, but no clean socks. I got no sheets, no pillow, or anything to clean the cell. On Wednesday, I scored nothing but a promise for toilet paper. No luck in getting a pencil, but I did get several sheets of writing paper plus one sack I took on the bus with me with legal paper and law notes. On Thursday, I finally got half a roll of toilet paper and let go. God, that felt good! I also scored a pencil, or I should say, half a pencil, no eraser, and so I'm now able to write. Luckily, I'd addressed an envelope before I left Folsom, since I haven't been able to get an envelope from anyone here. I have no news sources here, and don't know a soul. "B" Section is a mad house in the truest sense. Noise goes on all night, and a hand full of convicts run the section. The guards, I find are polite, and answer either "I don't know" or "yes," which is their way of getting you off their back. Like Tuesday, I asked a guard for some sheets, and he answered, "Sure," and that was it. Three cheers for psychology I! Tomorrow, I'll try and get this pencil sharpened, so I can write again, and I'll continue asking why I'm in isolation? Why I'm being punished, since I don't see how I could have a beef, I just got here. Committee met Tuesday, Wednesday and today, but I didn't go. I guess I'll go to court just as soon as they think up a charge, which might be anytime between now and

Christmas. Today, I did get some exercise, about 45 minutes, and as I stepped out side and smelled the salt air blowing over the bay, I suddenly felt better, knowing a world still existed outside. If any of you would like to come over and rap, I'd be most grateful, as I have no visitors, and until I get released from "B" Section, it will get lonely. My interests are writing, art and mathematics. I'm 43 years old, young in spirit, and dedicated to the revolution.

All Power To The People.
Your Brother, Harold W. Olsen

Folsom
February, 1971

Dear Sister and Sisters:

I want to thank you for your visit this past weekend, and tell you that you bring light and encouragement into a world that many times seems to appear as a void of eternal darkness. Thank you for showing me that human beings do exist.

My sister, as I sit and try to escape this verbal madness which presently surrounds me, I will try to the best of my ability to tell you some of those experiences which have occurred and taken place in my life and during my present incarceration. Try to forever bear in mind, Fay, that almost throughout the majority of my life, I have been living behind these steel bars and concrete walls. All of my teens have been spent confined within the California Youth Authority, while all of my twenties have been spent imprisoned in the California Adult Authority. I say this now as an explanation as to why my various forms of phraseology may be difficult to understand and how come some of my rambling may seem idle and the result of a demented or deteriorated mind; of which the latter may very well be true, as this type of mental conditioning is one of the best and major by-products of the California Penal and Judicial System. If anyone else had asked me to try and relay my personal adventures, I most probably would have avoided them as best I could, for I know it would

fall upon deaf ears, or at the very least misunderstood, but knowing and trusting you as I do, I believe that I can make some
semblance of an attempt, and feel that with you, it would be
understood.

First, I guess I had better start with my last appearance before
the Adult Authority Parole Board. I took the Parole Board 8½
years flat, a first termer, doing six months to ten years. I was
refused parole and my sentence was set at ten years. So I will
do every minute of the maximum of my sentence. Why was I
denied after doing so much time? Well, written on a little piece
of paper, the pig wrote that I could not be considered for parole,
because I was unstable. If this were really so, it seems ironic
that the pig anticipated my suddenly being stable as to the requirements of their standards, after being locked down in their
pits and cess pools, subjected to every indignity conceivable to
the human mind, for all my maturing years. Actually, they should
be proud of what they have created in my mind and body, for
surely nobody else could have built me as they have. But even
so, this is not why I was refused parole. While I was sitting there
before the Parole Board, the pig kept mentioning various "felony
beefs" that I have been accused of by other pigs while in prison,
but yet was never tried for. Some of these beefs I never heard
of before this day. Then I was accused of being a revolutionary
and Communist inspired, and that I had outside associations or
influences which are Communist inspired or party members. After
this I was pounced on for being white and affiliating myself with
black inmates. I was told that this is bad and was frowned upon
by Correctional Authorities and would create trouble within a
free society. Then I was asked about my homosexual alliances
and if I were a homosexual. I answered that I do not know if I
am a homosexual or not, because being locked up all of my life,
I've never had the opportunity to have a heterosexual relationship. The pig actually asked me what I meant by this, so I plainly
told him that I have never had any pussy, seen the same, touched
the same, or had any physical or sexual contact with a real
woman; but that from all of the stories I have heard, it sounds

pretty good. Even so, I could not say if I am homosexual or not without having a relationship with a woman and that I have throughout all of my life judged people as people and human beings without ever considering color or sex. The Board told me that these things are my problem and that I am a threat to society. I wonder if the Super Pigs have ever stopped to consider if they created this so-called problem? Yes, I believe they have, but their ignorance has told them that it just can't be helped, so it's my fault. That's cool, I like it.

Now I will try and break some of this down to its original form as best I can with real experiences and their causes.

On June 14, 1962, I was 19 years old and sent to State Prison, because I defended myself against a guy who was trying to kill me. I was mad and angry, because I knew that if I had enough money I would be free rather than locked up like some animal, but because I was poor and refused to submit to pig rules and desires, I was guilty before I ever went to trial. I picked up this case in the County Jail. The so-called victim was in jail for child molesting, parole violation and numerous other charges which were dropped. During the trial he was shown lying, all the D.A.'s witnesses testified for me, my witnesses were beautiful, no weapon was produced, everyone in the Court Room knew I should go free, including the jury, but the Judge instructed the jury to find me guilty, the jury asked to be reinstructed and again he instructed them to find me guilty and told them he goes home to eat at 5 p.m., so hurry up with the verdict. So I came to prison, and naturally I was angry. Because I was angry, I was considered mentally ill. I guess if I were happy or content, the pig would say I was programming. But how can a person like being in a cage? I don't like it and never will.

Because I was considered mentally ill, I spent my first 18 months on the hospital side of Vacaville. At first I gambled at cards a lot, had a few little fist fights, and a couple love affairs. Then one day the pig put me in the hole, saying they found contraband in my cell. One day I was in the hole, a therapist came by my cell while I was wearing nothing but my shorts, and asked me why I was locked up in segregation. All the while he was looking up and down my body, it got to the point that I didn't know, or could figure out, if the guy was talking to me or my shorts. Anyway, I ran it down to him and he finally split. A few weeks later Mr. Procunier told me that they found out someone else put the contraband in my cell, he gave me my back issues of canteen ducats and returned me to the main population. I asked my therapist about all of this, and he told me that someone became interested in me and started an investigation. I didn't find out until later just what that interest was. After I was back in the main line, I fell in love with a Puerto Rican homosexual. I was then brought up before the Classification Committee, and the pigs told me that they considered this person and I married and that he would be brought from his wing and moved into the same wing with me. At this time it was common practice for the pig to do this to prevent trouble created by jealousies. The pig said we could and would have freedom of sex, but if I broke any other rules, we would both go to isolation instead of one. Well, all was cool for awhile until my therapist had to leave and this guy I referred to earlier, was appointed my therapist. Dig, the first day he called me in and told me he was my therapist and being that I required individual therapy, we would have to probably use a cell for our sessions, then he smiled putting his arm around me. The next week he came to hold our therapy session in my lover's cell. What a scene that was. There I am, lying on the bed with this big ole pig sitting on the bed beside me. He asked me how was I doing, and when I told him I was doing fine, he started telling me how emotionally involved he was with me. Now Fay, remember, I am supposed to be mentally ill, so this sure did mess my mind up, because I couldn't figure out who was getting therapy. Me or this pig. About this time my lover come to the cell and politely terminated the session when he saw the pigs hand working its way up my lap. The next week was a re-run, but my friend kept on the scene to make sure things didn't get too out of line. Then, as this pig started to leave, he asked me if I was complexed or ashamed of my friend, whereby I pulled my lover to me and kissed him on the mouth, and told the therapist that I didn't believe in make believe, but accepted life, good or bad, and was proud of my role. That theraputic pig's mind sure was fucked up. The next week he wanted my lover and I to perform various sex acts while he and a female co-therapist watched me. Now, Fay, the guy was just going too far, and so I told him he would have to go somewhere else for that. Anyway, the next few weeks I hid from him. Then one day a black inmate was hurt and he said he got hurt while trying to break up a fight between myself and another inmate. About this time, along comes my Cinderella Therapist who has the audacity to tell me that is nothing, for nobody worries about niggers, and you know Fay, the next day Procunier said the very same thing, never asking me if I did hurt the guy or why, in fact I didn't even go to the hole. Well a couple weeks went by and I finally told Cinderella to hit it, that I didn't want to see him no more because the way things were doing, something serious was going to happen, that he didn't move me in any way, and that it was repulsive to me that a guy as fucked as him had control of the lives of so many people.

A few weeks later I was transferred to San Quentin. Being a great big old naive fool, I tried to go home by doing clean time, and was subsequently stabbed ten days later. After I got out of the hospital, I was put in the Adjustment Center and was told by the pig, that I was a dog for getting holes punched in my body. While in A.C. the pig threw a note in a Black's cell, calling him a nigger and saying that he had better not come out of his cell, or he would be killed. The pig then came to my cell and in a loud voice told me not to throw any more threatening notes in negro cells. Sister, this is only a minor criss-cross the pig uses, but think of its many potentials when applied in a place containing extremely high racial tensions, along with the ever present thought that people are always telling on one another. It's minor, but it is explosive and has caused many a man to die. Anyway, this was my introduction to San Quentin. I was brought before the Parole Board at about this time and was denied a year for being the victim of a stabbing. After the Board, I was brutally beaten and tortured by the pigs in A.C. In fact, they hurt me so bad I was in the hospital eleven days on the critical list. As you know, I proved this to a jury, that I was the victim of Cruel and Unusual Punishment in Federal Court, but the pig Parole Board denied me 2 more years for the pigs beating me up. This is the starting of my awareness of the functions and power of the Adult Authority. Then and their policy is, fuck the law, the convict's a dog, he has no human rights, and the pig Board is the law.

Fay, during my 3½ year stay in San Quentin, I witnessed many atrocities that would take forever to tell, if I were to write by hand a complete description of each instance. So I will now tell you of a few of the ones that I personally saw or witnessed myself in one form or another, that may show to a degree, some of the pigs real everyday nature, and possibly their effect upon the convict will be clearly evident to the eyes of the most deceived John Doe citizen. Like for example, one time a bunch of us were locked up in the Adjustment Center, when late one night the pigs brought a guy in and locked him up. Later on, about midnight they went off into his cell, but we didn't hear any noise, so we thought the guy was sick or something. After the pig left, we tried to call him, but we couldn't get a response, so we all went to sleep. The next morning, over 8 hours later, some pigs on the next shift, along with a doctor, opened the guy's cell, and when they brought him out, we could see his eye balls on his cheeks, his tongue on his chest, his face purple, and the Doctor said rigor mortis has set in and that the guy had been dead over 8 hours. The night before, the pigs counted at least four separate times, and the pig had served each man his breakfast, but yet no pig saw this guy.

Throughout my early stay in Quentin, I was always being told by the pig about race hating niggers. One time I was on the main line, a black and white got into a hassel head up, the white guy lost and was minus a lung. The pig held what he called an investigation and questioned everyone who was out on the tier at the time of the hassel. A pig told me that they knew a black was involved, and if a nigger came up dead, they wouldn't miss him, but for me not to do anything he wouldn't do. Knowing by now that he would do anything, I knew then that I had a license to kill a black. Later on as the pig learned I had close associations and affiliations with black inmates, they started referring to me as "that nigger-lover" and a race agitator. I guess they were mad because they had given me my license to kill and I didn't punch holes in the required quota of blacks. Several times blacks have come up to me and explained how the pig pulled them aside and ran down that I was an agitator and that my race would be better off without me and that it would save blacks a lot of trouble if I were eliminated. In short, the pig was trying to get a brother to kill me.

During my years in Quentin I had some very beautiful experiences, and too some very terrible ones. But most important of my lessons at this time was my learning just how deadly and ruthless the pig is, and the many devious and nefarious tactics he employs to pit one race against the other, to create and agitate a continuous state of chaos, dissension and turmoil amongst the convicts, and how he uses these conditions to control each man, and greatest of all, that if your white and have black friends your a piece of shit.

How do I smell, sis? Maybe when they blow me away you can use my body for fertilizer.

But the pig fucked up with me, because I was and still am, determined to stand by my comrades and friends, for it was evident then as it is now, that every minute of the day, their lives are endangered by the pig machine. About this time, 40 pigs vamped on four brothers and I for testifying on behalf of a black man the pig had framed. After this I was transferred to Folsom's A.C. Fay, when or after I got to Folsom, you should have seen my personal property when I got it. Written across all of my letters were words or phrases such as "You niggerloving punk, your going to die" and "Suck my dick nigger lover," and written across all my pictures were words like, "Did your nigger friends fuck her too?" and various other sayings to this effect, and phallic symbols drawn across them. They had written on everything their little pens could scribble on. Sister this was how I was introduced to my new pig slave-master and how come I no longer have any pictures. This is your modern penal rehabilitative program. Society is making some kind of progress.

For a long time here, it was just one Black brother and I against all of A.C., but our love and brotherhood for one another downed the pigs many traps, our unity and soul surpassed their criss-cross and kept us above and ahead of the shallow ignorance of the cons who were unknowingly being used by the pig as a weapon against us. We spoke to nobody but each other, we exchanged things with no one but each other, and therefore we are alive today. The pig finally put him on the main line and then a month later they went and told all my friends that I refused to come to the main-line, that I was a coward and snitched on all of them. Then they went to my enemies (which were many) and told them I was coming out to the mainline the next day, what time I was being released, and what door I could come out of. The next day I went to the main-line, both of my arms holding property, set up like a duck. But feeling something was wrong, I immediately placed my property on the ground by the wall just outside the A.C. door. I saw a guy I knew and had him go get my friend, then I had another guy to help me. My friend came immediately and told me what the pig had done the day before, so from there on out, we were ready, together as one. That night some so-called enemies locked up for protection. The next day, Lieutenant C. of custody had me locked up again and said it was a mistake my being in the general population, because a guy I had assaulted in the County Jail was on the mainline, and that the guy said there would be a race war if he and I were kept on the line together. That's a lie. The pig sent me out there hoping some violent madness would start, but when the pigs' friends got scared, they locked me up.

Five days later I was transferred. First I went to the hole in D.V.I., and to "O" wing in Soledad, where the pig already had the table set to kill me and one of my black brothers. We were told about this the first day we got there. Three days later my black brother and comrade was murdered in front of my cell while we were talking. I was locked inside, he was standing on the tier, the pig refused to let us out at the same time, knowing that if they did it would be death to their cowardly little tools. The pigs thought my comrade's death was real funny, and a month later a pig was standing outside my cell bars and started joking about my dead comrade, so I spit on him and was taken to isolation. A week later I was taken back to Folsom's Adjustment Center. The pig on my return to Folsom, said that I will have to be kept locked up because they felt I may be angry over my comrade's death and want to retaliate.

Fay, I could and will later on, write you of numerous incidents that have occurred all the way up until now, where the pig has shown his highest form of piggishness, such as when they poisoned me, when they tried to shoot me, tried to shoot air into the vein of my arm, when they tried to beat me to death, tried to get convicts on different occasions to kill me, tried to give me murder beefs, but as I said, I will tell them later in full detail if you want to hear them.

Right now, I wish to discuss a little bit what the political situation of the convicts and the pigs, as it exists today in these prison converted concentration camps. In prison today, you have according to the pig, a convict, a inmate, and a revolutionary. I have the esteemed honor of being classified, by my pig captor, as the latter. Whether he is right or wrong is here nor there. The fact is that this creates a very pertinent situation, especially as the pig has bluntly told me in the presence of others that I am a revolutionary and that it is out-right war between them and myself and my fellow comrades and friends. Really the pig is a fool to say this, for now he just makes us more aware and cautious, building our solidarity. The other day, the pig tried to install fear by killing a white revolutionary brother, then the next day they rat packed a black revolutionary brother, then a white one, then a black one. But, as I said, he is a fool, for he is only making us stronger and killing himself. This crude forwardness has opened many eyes to his pig ideology, therefore he has not been able to shoot any revolutionary brothers on the exercise yard. Maybe we should thank him.

I have about 16 more months for a discharge from Reagan's slave camps, so I should be pretty well educated and prepared to serve the cause and help you and the people who have been struggling all of these years to give everyone an equal chance and opportunity, and maybe help educate some of those who are still in the dark and dominated by pig indoctrination. The pig says I will be dead before sixteen months, and other convicts and comrades say the same, or that the pig will set me up and give me some more time. This is all very probable, it has been done before, so I want to be the first nor the last, but either way, I want it to mean something. That's one reason I hope maybe you and people such as yourself may be able to prevent others from being subjected to these. My sister, I am a revolutionary and believe in revolution with all my heart, for Fay, my sister, I know and see every day the pig and the turds of his mind. Everyday, the pig tells me how my comrades and I will never be free, and you know, so far he has proved it, for anyone with any soul or spirit is continually locked down, harassed and eventually murdered. What a waste, for really some of the strongest and most potential men of this country and era, are being kept in these concentration camps for the rest of their lives. But as I said, the pig is making us stronger and larger and maybe eventually we can demand our freedom and rights of men.

My sister, I know you don't receive any money for helping us, and I see your finger nails wore down to the wick from slaving for us. At this time there is little I or my comrades can do for you, but I have sent you a check for $20 which you should get now or soon, and I want you to take it and buy you and your husband or Patti a dinner and rest or at least relax for awhile. Do this for me and those of us who love you and the people.

Right on, and all power to the people.

Your Comrade and Friend

Sherman J. Warner

The following letter reveals the black convicts' concern that a lawyer who corresponded with whites might not be trustworthy.

Folsom
12-31-70

Dear Comrades:

In a little while this seemingly nonsense marking of time will bring a new year. But all its trimmings will be very old. Perhaps we'll start everything over again after Victory.

What's happening is, your letter to a brother on the other [white] side gave an avenue for some to vent there frustration. They questioned you. But don't be sad. A lot of people are still accustomed to misdirecting their energy. Because no suit has been filed, and you ask for more information. They cry! Knowing they have said all there is. And with nothing more to add, the feeling of powerfulness comes out perverted. It's a bad scene to see men reduced to children—who need protection. Like the little boy who think his father can whip the World. One day he must face reality. These are the changes those who Cry are going through.

I enjoyed our last visit. More than the rest. I am smiling. You are crazy. No you are really a nice person. I wish I knew more like yourself.

Doc

FOLSOM HANGING

On January 6, 1971, William Thornton committed suicide in a Folsom Prison strip cell. The clouded circumstances that led to his death have provoked men still incarcerated in the prison to make this incident known outside. Excerpts from their letters follow; details differ, but the main facts do not.

A black inmate writes:

By now you have received several letters describing the death of Thornton here in 4/A. It was murder. But this time it was done through negligence and intimidation. Of course the omnipotent officials have no one who will question what has been called suicide. If there was the slightest investigation I'm sure the incident would take on a new look.

There is no doubt he was driven from the rim of sanity by "fear." Which climaxed in him hanging himself. An ironical paradox when you understand. He wanted to live so desperately that the thought of being killed snapped his mind. Odd. But not really, if you could have seen the hours leading to his death. Even I thought they were back there trying to kill him. Perhaps they would have if he hadn't did it himself.

All morning the Pigs were coming and going from his cell. He had become so frightened by then, he had barricaded himself in. His intentions then, were to protect himself against any moves by the Pigs. Around 10:00 a.m., the prison's psychiatrist passed through on his once-a-week round. He saw Thornton. And in less than five minutes. He saw the completely deranged state Thornton was in. And apparently made a request to have him moved to the Psychiatry ward. This was not done. Instead the goons put their heads together, and came up with some more shit.

Around 1:00 p.m.—after most of the people on this side were let out for yard—Pigs B. and M. went back to the strip cell where Thornton was. B. was carrying a 14 or 15″ inch screwdriver-like piece. About 10 minutes passed. And Pig counselor B. joined the others. What they were doing we couldn't really see. There is an enclosure on those cells. But Thornton began to scream "Help they are trying to kill me."

Several of us after hearing this began calling the pigs and making noise in general. The Pigs came out of the enclosure A after five minutes. Two stood outside the door and one went to get something he concealed under his clothing. It was probably the saw they later came out with. All together they were in the front section of his cell over an hour. By then it was time for them to bring in the inmates exercising in the yard.

From the way the Pigs talked and acted it did indeed seem they were planning to kill him. To a paranoid mind there could be no doubt that this was what they were going to do.

While the Pigs was bringing the yard in he hung himself. The only reason I'm sure they didn't hang him is: He was still alive —sitting on the side of his bed—when the first few comrades came in from the yard. One of his friends saw him. If it wasn't for that fact, I would have believed they hung him themselves.

When the yard was finished coming in, the Pigs went back to his cell—neither of them went right in. B. called up front for the head Pig. Notice there is no great effort to get him down. Which by the way he was hung right beneath the tray slot. About ten minutes later the man was brought out very much dead.

A white inmate states:

I was informed today by a convict who overheard the psych doctor tell these pigs in medical terms Thornton was out of it and for him to be removed from the strip cell he was in, to the psych ward in the hospital immediately. This took place in the morning.

In the afternoon when the yard was out, (least amount of convicts to witness their action) they proceeded in there most piggish manner being totally unskilled and trained in how to handle such psych cases, let the man hang himself while they antagonized him to this act.

A chicano inmate comments:

(A) prisoner by the name of William Thornton committed *suicide?* by hanging in a strip cell. Note: the news cast merely said a prisoner committed suicide *in Folsom Prison*; no mention of the strip cell. He was about 26 yrs. of age, and was to go home, I believe some time in *March* of this year. I was told that he had called for, and told the psychiatrist, K., that he could not take the strip cell that he wanted out; and that K. replied that "there's nothing wrong with you," and then he left. You wonder why I get so frustrated in here—pigs, filthy pigs using psychological cruelty to murder by suicide and there's no way I can prevent it.

A white inmate writes:

On Wednesday 6, 1971, an inmate housed in a strip cell here in 4-A hung himself. What makes this warrant attention is the extenuating circumstances surrounding this incident. The inmate's name was Wm. Thornton, age 33. He was scheduled to be released February 15, 1971. Thornton was *not* a problem inmate custody wise, disciplinary wise, or politically.

He felt loneliness, anxiety, and despair, which these sprawling confines breed. Being close to a release he naturally was wired up nervously, anxious for his upcoming date. He requested several times to talk with the institution psychiatrist, Doctor M., but was refused. Thornton had a problem and requested help, but they wouldn't give it to him.

So, for what reasons he had, who knows but him, he hung himself from a ventilator. This incident happened during the period of day when the pig was releasing the tier he was on for their hours exercise on the yard. The pigs found him hanging, and could of saved him. But they walked off and left him hanging til they continued running all the inmates out to the yard. After they ran the yard they came back and cut him down. Naturally he was dead now. But he wasn't when they found him first, then left.

I've seen them (fellow inmates) killed, shot down, beat unmercifully with their hands cuffed. I've been beat, thrown down stairs, and had false charges put on me. What can we do?

Not only are we brutalized mentally and physically, years taken from our lives, but we are shot and crippled or killed at will. And we can't do anything about it, we're helpless.

POWER TO THE PEOPLE!

Folsom
December 24, 1970

Dearest Mom & Dad:

Well its Christmas Eve—"and all through my cell, not a creature is stirring, except maybe a mouse, or two, or three—smile."

I am spending this Christmas in a room called the "hole"—this condition is the result of what the authorities claimed was a minor rule infraction. I will also be spending the New Year in this room—it's all a part of the prison's idea of Christmas spirit. It is quiet here, and pretty dark—but I am imprisoned only in body—my mind remains free and it will supply me with reasons to retain the Christmas spirit. A belief in the future sure helps in this regard.

I was just interrupted by a jailer and his flashlight. He was making his rounds, counting his prisoners. I wished him a Merry Christmas—but he just slammed the heavy steel door and trampled off down the corridor rattling his keys. I am sure that he thought that my remark was just a method of mocking him and his job—but it was sincerely meant: For who but a person like he needs a greeting of good cheer? It's impossible to hate a person like him—he requires pity for with him its a matter of having a free body—but a imprisoned mind and spirit—For how else could a person accept a job wherein he is paid his silver at the expense of so many others misery?

Your check arrived tonight—too late for Christmas, but I will be able to buy some food items next week—and that will help because people put in the hole are put on reduced food rations— the inmates in the hole call the stuff they feed us in here, a dog bisket. It's made by pressing left over foods into a block and then drying it out. I don't eat the stuff—not solely because of pride, but because of the smell. But I am saving up some of the crumbs for a little cockroach that I am trying to tame. He is a smart little fellow and a good holiday companion. It's too bad that he can't appreciate the little Christmas tree that I drew on the wall. When I am allowed to buy some food items I will buy him a piece of cheese as a Christmas gift.

Things might work out next February—but I am not holding out much hope—I have so often in the past—only to be disappointed. Tomorrow I will try not to think of homes filled full of bright lights and happy people, that will only make me sad. I will also try to hide my worry and concern for my children at the back of my mind, instead I will think of you and Dad, and be happy with such good thoughts. So my Christmas Cheer will be the result of such wonderful parents and the equally wonderful memory of them.

I will also spend my Christmas thinking of a man born on this day so long ago. I will think of all that he taught and wonder why so many people talk about what he taught but live out their lives by the rules of his tempter.

I have spent a great deal of time researching the history of Christ. Jim the Chaplain here has supplied me with over 100 books on this subject. More than anything else I have come to see the great difference in what he taught and the way the people who claim to follow him live. Because of this I respect him, but I will never recognize the religions who have betrayed his word. I cannot respect people who talk love, peace, forgiveness, and practice hate, greed, and selfishness. All in all I will have a happy Christmas, Thanks To Both Of You,

Love, Wayne

P.S. My pet cockroach sends his best wishes.

Dear Comrades:

After pondering the discussion we had concerning the term "prison reform" I have concluded that more people will support our cause and you will avoid apathy by centering your efforts around the title that has already been established "political prisoners." The title carries the immediate aim of prisoners for humanity and justice. . . . The word "justice" should be emphasized and must be recognized by the people; justice is the word that indicates our goal.

What I want to get across is that it would be reactionary to our position here to support the rambunctious call for prison reform, and I think this term should be defined to the people—all people. You can even go as far as to call it a dirty word; in order to resolve this issue and move forward to further progress we must analyze the term "prison reform" and its fundamental objective; it has but one implication—overhaul. That means changing the frame on the wall—but not the picture itself. On one hand it brings into existence a new policy of administrative control, the order of old rules and regulations are re-organized and formulated to fit a new pacification program, this program is designed and regulated to pacify inmates by offering them a movie, a new radio station a new and freshly painted cell, bars included. But no immediate parole, in short the objective is to keep the inmate happy and the assembly lines rolling. On the other hand it maintains the use of weapon control (changing the frame but not the picture); it carries out the use of tear gas, billy clubs, pick handles, the sweat box, solitary lock-up, and the use of 30/30 automatic rifles.

This process of dehumanization, this method of psychological repression, the open physical attacks against inmates by sadistic guards, all take on a moderate tone, and inmates are taken behind closed doors, for inmates who have over a period of years attempted to expose the blatant atrocities of U.S. concentration camps, are inmates who are classified a threat to the system based on their political ideology. These inmates are forced to live in the sediment and filth of solitary lock-up for protesting prison conditions—they are forgotten, castigated, no parole and the wheels of vengeance, retaliation, and injustice run full speed ahead . . . Beyond this, prison reform obstructs, falsifies, misleads, attacks and oppresses the call for abolishing U.S. neo-concentration camps.

My friend, there are many people who hold mis-conceptions about prisons and the type of people inside them. The existing prison system has a long and rampant history of falsifying, evading, covering up and hiding their unlawful activities from the eyes and ears of the people. This, however, results from a pathological prison administration who tells lies and never tells the truth at all; the aftermath being the catalyst motivating the unaware to take sides with the system, rather than the victims of the system.

In prison we are governed and controlled by force—there is force all around us, above us. Force is the weapon used against the people's will. Here inside the concentration camp we are . . . forced . . . into . . . resisting . . . force!!

Along with many people who are locked up here I acknowledge the fact that there are many sincere people with good intentions who have rendered their time and efforts in trying to reveal the foul conditions existing here in San Quentin as well as other prisons in this state.

Our only hope lies in the people's endeavor to hear our protest and support our cause. Building more and better prisons is not the solution, build a thousand prisons, arrest and lock up tens of thousands of people; all to no avail. This will not arrest poverty, oppression, and the other ills of this unjust social order. We need people who will stand up and speak out when it is a matter of right or wrong, of justice or injustice, or struggling or not struggling to help correct and remove conditions affecting the people. All I ask is that the people support us, I will break my back in helping bring peace and justice upon the face of the Earth.

John Cluchette

SOLEDAD

In 1966, Robert Charles Jordan, a black prisoner at Soledad, charged Superintendent Cletus Fitzharris with cruel and unusual punishment. The decision of the court in this case was unusual in two respects: the court intervened in the internal administration of a prison, and it accepted as true the testimony of the convict plaintiff and convict witnesses rather than that of prison officials. The judge, George B. Harris, himself visited the prison and inspected the strip cells where Jordan had been confined.

Despite the court's verdict of cruel and unusual punishment, Fitzharris remained in charge of Soledad, where he served until the summer of 1971, when he was promoted to deputy director of the California Department of Corrections.

Excerpts from Jordan's complaint follow.

Robert Charles JORDAN, Jr., Plaintiff,

v.

C. J. FITZHARRIS et al., Defendants.
No. 44786
United States District Court
N. D. California, S. D.
September 6, 1966
257 F. Supp. 674

MEMORANDUM OPINION AND ORDER
GEORGE B. HARRIS, Chief Judge.

. . . Plaintiff's cruel and unusual punishment contention arises out of his confinement from July 9 until July 20, 1965, in a so-called "strip cell" at Soledad. . . .

. . . The Amended complaint filed by Jordan, through his appointed counsel, particularized his grievances . . .

On or about July 9, 1965, plaintiff was placed in a special punishment unit at the Correctional Training Facility, known as a "strip cell" (hereinafter referred to as "strip cell"). Plaintiff was continuously confined in solitary confinement in said strip cell for twelve consecutive days.

*   *   *   *   *   *   *   *   *   *

During plaintiff's confinement in said strip cell, plaintiff was forced to remain in said strip cell with said flaps and door of the second wall closed. As a result, plaintiff was deprived of light and ventilation for twelve days, except that twice a day the door of the second wall was opened for approximately fifteen minutes.

The interior of said strip cell is without any facilities, except that there is a raised concrete platform at the rear of the cell containing a hole to receive bodily wastes. There is no mechanism within the cell for "flushing" bodily wastes from this hole. "Flushing" is controlled by personnel of the Correctional Training Facility from the exterior of said strip cell. The hole was only "flushed" at approximately 8:30 a.m. and 9:00 p.m. on some of the twelve days plaintiff was confined in said strip cell.

During plaintiff's confinement in said strip cell, the strip cell was never cleaned. As a result of the continuous state of filth to which plaintiff was subjected, plaintiff was often nauseous and vomited, and the vomit was never cleaned from the plaintiff's cell. When plaintiff was first brought to the strip cell, the floor and walls of the strip cell were covered with the bodily wastes of previous inhabitants of the strip cell . . .

Plaintiff was forced to remain in said strip cell for twelve days without any means of cleaning his hands, body or teeth. No means was provided which could enable plaintiff to clean any part of his body at any time. Plaintiff was forced to handle and eat his food without even the semblance of cleanliness or any provision for sanitary conditions.

For the first eight days of plaintiff's confinement in said strip cell, plaintiff was not permitted clothing of any nature and was forced to remain in said strip cell absolutely naked. Thereafter, plaintiff was given a pair of rough overalls only.

Plaintiff was forced to remain in said strip cell with no place to sleep but upon the cold concrete floor of the strip cell, except that a stiff canvas mat approximately 4½ feet by 5½ feet was provided. Said mat was so stiff that it could not be folded to cover plaintiff without such conscious exertion by plaintiff that sleep was impossible. Plaintiff is six feet and one inch tall and could not be adequately covered by said stiff canvas mat even when holding said mat over himself. The strip cell was not heated during the time that plaintiff was forced to remain there.

Plaintiff is informed and believes and on that basis alleges that plaintiff has been and may be subjected to confinement in said strip cell without the authorization of the Superintendent, the Deputy Superintendent, the Associate Superintendent, or anyone of comparable administrative rank; that lower-rank personnel of the Correctional Training Facility purport to have exercised and intend to exercise in the future broad discretion in confining plaintiff in said strip cell; that said lower-rank personnel purport to have the discretion to confine plaintiff in said strip cell for 60 consecutive days; and that there are no standards for the proper exercise of such discretion.

On many occasions prior to July 9, 1965, plaintiff has been confined in said strip cell, plaintiff is continually living under the threat of repeated confinement in said strip cell, and plaintiff is constantly subject to confinement in said strip cell pursuant to purported disciplinary procedures as they presently exist and will continue to exist unless enjoined by this Court.

Plaintiff has been denied adequate medical care prior to, during, and subsequent to said confinement in said strip cell, despite repeated oral and written requests for same made in good faith by or on behalf of plaintiff.

Prior to and subsequent to said confinement in said strip cell, plaintiff has been forced to endure confinement in "O Wing" of the Correctional Training Facility without adequate protection from the raw outdoor elements, in that plaintiff's cell front offers no protection from the elements, being only bars, there are no window panes for the large window openings in the outside wall of the corridor which is directly outside plaintiff's cell, and there is insufficient artificial heat, if any, to combat the outdoor climatic conditions which prevail in plaintiff's cell.

Jordan, called as a witness on his own behalf, gave testimony which fortified the foregoing allegations. He testified categorically concerning the practices engaged in by the defendants. He was subjected to a lengthy and searching cross-examination by the two attorneys representing the defendants. His testimony is clear and convincing. (Tr. p. 368, *et. seq.*)

More particularly, Jordan discharged the burden cast upon him with respect to the period of time he was confined in the strip cell; the fact that he was deprived of clothing for the period of time, at least for seven days; that he was required to sleep on a strong blanket ill adapted to the uses for which it was put; that the flaps were closed practically all of the time thus depriving him of both light and adequate ventilation in the cell; that the elements of cleanliness were likewise deprived him, to-wit, water, soap, towel, tooth brush, toothpaste, implements for cleaning the cell, and shower. (Tr. p. 378, *et seq.*)

It is evident from the foregoing narrative of Jordan's testimony

that he was required to eat the meager prison fare in the stench
and filth that surrounded him, together with the accompanying
odors that ordinarily permeated the cell. Absent the ordinary
means of cleansing his hands preparatory to eating, it was suggested by the prison consulting psychiatrist, Dr. Hack, that he
might very well use toilet paper for this purpose plus his small
ration of water, being two cups a day. (Tr. p. 597.)

. . . On behalf of the plaintiff, the following inmate witnesses
were called: Alfonso Esparza, Herman Alexander, Melvin Alli-
son, Wendell Harris, Siegfried Porte and Warren Wells . . .

It is to be observed that the inmates and their testimony were
subjected to vigorous and searching cross-examination. Notwithstanding such scrutiny, the narratives contain the essentials of
truth and are credible and convincing.

. . . .

(8) Usually the administrative responsibility of correctional
institutions rests peculiarly within the province of the officials
themselves, without attempted intrusion or intervention on the
part of the courts . . .

(9) However, when, as it appears in the case at bar, the
responsible prison authorities in the use of the strip cells have
abandoned elemental concepts of decency by permitting conditions to prevail of a shocking and debased nature, then the courts
must intervene—and intervene promptly—to restore the primal
rules of a civilized community in accord with the mandate of
the Constitution of the United States . . .

(10) In the opinion of the court, the type of confinement de-
picted in the foregoing summary of the inmates' testimony results in a slow-burning fire of resentment on the part of the
inmates until it finally explodes in open revolt, coupled with their
violent and bizarre conduct. Requiring man or beast to live, eat
and sleep under the degrading conditions pointed out in the
testimony creates a condition that inevitably does violence to
elemental concepts of decency.

The testimony further reflects that the security officers made no effort to remedy the situation, notwithstanding persistent and violent complaints on the inmates' part . . .

The graphic testimony of the psychiatrist, Dr. Raymond L. Hack, . . . reads, in part, as follows:

THE COURT: All right, Doctor, will you pause for a moment and consider yourself inside one of the cells in question with the flaps up. Do you concede that there isn't any light in the cell, Doctor?

THE WITNESS: Yes.

THE COURT: It is absolutely dark.

THE WITNESS: Not quite, because these are not, as the so-called solitary confinement cells of former years, where there was no light. There is a slight seepage of light.

THE COURT: Very slight.

THE WITNESS: Very slight.

THE COURT: Mindful of the conditions under which a man is confined in a cell in question, how do you propose he maintain his personal bodily cleanliness, his hands and the like?

THE WITNESS: He is provided with—is provided with the toilet tissue. He is supposed to be removed to be—he is supposed to be removed to be showered.

THE COURT: When? And how often?

THE WITNESS: I believe at least every five days was the minimum.

THE COURT: So for a period of five days, at least, his body, if he is stripped, and his hands equally, would be the subject of some degree of contamination. Isn't that correct?

THE WITNESS: Yes, but as—

THE COURT: Is it correct, Doctor, or is it not?

THE WITNESS: For a period of five days he possibly might be quite soiled.

THE COURT: Yes. And quite contaminated.

THE WITNESS: Yes. . . .

THE COURT: Is it not true, notwithstanding the stench

or smell, many of these inmates were permitted to and forced to eat their meals in that stench and odor?

THE WITNESS: I don't know as they were forced to. It is true that if they were going to eat, that they might have to eat under those circumstances.

* * * * * * * * * *

"There were, it is true, some minor changes in certain procedures as they relate to the strip cells. But the changes were only slight physical adjustments to the mandates of the court order. The strip cells are still such that a human being should not be made to undergo incarceration in one. They are still dirty, they are still poorly ventilated, they are still poorly heated and in most cases the lighting provided is deliberately not turned on by the pigs. The amount of exercise allowed inmates confined in a strip cell would not keep the muscles and body of a year-old baby in tone and in good health. The open mouth toilets are still smelly and the inmate must still eat his food within the same space, within 5 feet of the smelly, nauseous fumes arising from the toilet. It does not sound too bad when you say it or read it, but I would like to record the reaction of the average citizen of the U.S. to the suggestion that he or she eat 7 days a week, 3 times a day in their family bathroom. The situation is further compounded by the fact that the toilets in the strip cells are communal in nature and the previous user may have been infected with an highly infectious disease. The toilets are never given any disinfectant treatment, nor are inmates provided with any, only with scouring powder.

The psychological aspects of the strip cells are unchanged. Strip cells were and are designed with one purpose in mind; to break the will and spirit of the inmate subjected to incarceration in such a cell. *Not* to "control" the inmate. *Not* to "quiet down" an inmate. *Not* to prevent an inmate from harming himself. *Not* to prevent an inmate from agitating others. But purely and simply to *break* the inmate's will. To *break* the inmate's spirit."

Jordan

EXHIBIT A
Statement of Facts

Soledad Central, Calif.

I swear on my life and on those who have perished unmercifully under the cruel hands of these racial anti-Black officials, that what you are about to read is the pure, honest truth and nothing but:

To All (Blacks) Concerned:

(1969) On October the 27th, Eugene Grady, Eddie Whiteside and myself (Hugo Pinell), were transferred to Soledad Correctional Institution Facility, from Folsom Prison. We were place in the Max Row section of O-Wing. Immediately entering the Sallyport area of the section, I could hear inmates shouting and making remarks such as; "Nigger is a scum low down dog, etc." I couldn't believe my ears at first because I know if I could hear these things, the officers beside me could too and I started wondering what was going on(?). Then, I fixed my eyes on the Wing Sergeant and I began to see the clear picture of why those inmates didn't care if the officials heard them instigating racial conflict. The Sergeant was and still is Mr. M., a known prejudice character towards Blacks because of previous unforgettable experiences with Blacks. I was placed in cell #139 and since that moment up until now I have had no peace of mind. The white inmates made it a 24 hour job of cursing Black Inmates just for kicks and the officials harassed us with consistency also. On October the 28th, my personal property was handed to me and I only received one third of what I had in Folsom, plus it was torn along

148

with half of the photographs they allowed me to have. But, I still kept collectively at ease. Soon, on November the 12th, they had the first shake down since I was there. The officials went straight to Whiteside's cell and I didn't believe my eyes at how they operated. They only went in the cell for seconds while Whiteside was hand-cuffed in another cell. They came out and without a cause, took Whiteside to the other side of O-Wing which is considered Isolation. I asked the officers where they were taking Whiteside and one of them told me to shut-up. About two minutes they came back and shook my cell down and I figured they would take me to the other side also, but they didn't!! They only accused me of having a torn sheet in my cell and they charged me $1.26 for it. In their records shows that the set of sheets on my bed were untouched, so I asked them how they came about with a torn sheet and again I was told to shut-up and was given ten (10) days cell exercise which means I don't come out of my cell for ten days! I still didn't say anything. The next day, I got a visit in a visiting room and when I came back, inmate Meneweather (a Black) told me that the police had attacked W. L. Nolen (a Black) while being hand-cuffed and he had been taken to Isolation! Now, this was a little too much to accept, so Edwards (a Black), Meneweather and myself protested accordingly to their ways; we threw some liquid on officer D. since he was the cause of W. L. Nolen getting attacked. We didn't have any meanings of defense. No one knew how we were doing down here, so, we could only respond in protection of each other! They came back and threw gas in our cells until we almost died—seriously—I had to wave a towel since I was choking from the gas. They told me that they wouldn't open the door until I undressed, back up to the door and stick my arms out. I did just that, they hand-cuffed me and dragged me to the other side, naked. Meneweather and Edwards received the same treatment. We were placed in the so called strip-cells in the back of the tier. The next day the doctor came by, not specially to see us, but mainly making his once a week routine. He asked me if I was okay and I told him, "yeah," I'm alright. I wanted to say "No sir, my eyes and skin are burning from the gas," but I couldn't do it because I didn't have any hopes of getting help from anyone except my own people. Then, we were given 29 days isolation, including 15 days R.D. (Restricted Diet). This R.D. is served twice a day and believe me, even a dog wouldn't eat it, perhaps not even a pig! In that dark cell I did a lot of thinking on what all this harassment would lead to because surely, the officials could see how well together we were and we didn't let the White inmate's fat-mouthing affect us in the least. Then, my visits were restricted to the Captain's Office and I kept cool because all my brothers were being mistreated, some worse then me. For instance; W. L. Nolen was disliked by all the officials and what angers me is that, these officials don't hide it, they just come out in the open and let you know, you are not appreciated in O-Wing if you are Black. After our 29 days were over we returned to Max Row but before that they had brought inmate Grady to Isolation trying to frame him also—I asked him why they (officials) did so many petty things and he said he couldn't understand it either but in our eyes we could see the answer— we were Black and we weren't fooling ourselves, we merely try to give each other encouragement. When we came back to Max Row (Edwards, Meneweather, and myself) Whiteside and Nolen were already back. Again we layed back and accepted the insults from White Inmates. These officials didn't allow no one to exercise except inmates of their own race in group of three at one time—so that no mexican, white or black inmate came in contact with one another at any time. They violated this rule by letting whites and mexicans exercise together and get haircuts on the same day so that this way it made it obvious what they meant to plant in people's mind by segregating Blacks from everybody else.

So, it was no secret that racial tension existed on Max Row day in and day out. By this time, it was close to Christmas and Blacks were housing as follows; Nolen (#134), Satcher (#144), Whiteside (#140), Myself, Pinell (#139), Randolph (#137), Meneweather (#134), Edwards (#132), Miller (#130), and Anderson (#126). Anderson was harassed the next day (around the 16th of Dec.) and taken to Isolation. On the 18th day, Nance (a Black) was brought in from Isolation and placed in cell #128. That same day I was informed by officials that I was to go to Sacramento County Jail, the next day. I couldn't figure out what would be the reason for me going to Sacramento. So, on the 19th, before I left, Grady was returned to Max Row and house in #127. Now, we were all wondering why all of the sudden so many Blacks were being moved on our side, because, really, when I first came on this tier, there were only four (4) Blacks (Nolen, Meneweather, Edwards and Anderson) and they have been there for quite a while putting up with officials, as well as inmates' insults. The only thing we had going for us, was ourselves, and we behaved so civilized that it enraged everyone to try more mischievous plots against us hoping we would react savagely as they did, but without triumph! Anyway, on the 19th I left for Sacramento, it was a Friday and I didn't return until Tuesday the 23rd. I was put in the same cell #139. It was the same environment—the air stayed stuffed with "Nigger here, and Nigger there."

On the 28th of Dec., a list was passed out announcing the opening of the Max Row yard on the 29th. But it didn't open because there was still some work yet to be done. But I did notice that white inmates and officials were awfully cheerful for some reason or another and they continuously didn't forget to remind us of the yard opening soon. Nolen kept telling me that these officials were up to no good and the white inmates would pass my cell asking me, "are you coming out when the yard opens?"— most of the time I would laugh at them and sometimes I would just sigh and roll on my other side trying to sleep.

Days went by and on Monday the 12th, I left for Sacramento County Jail again. It was raining like hell up that way so I figured the weather was the same at Soledad. Tuesday morning I was taken to Court, but someone said it was a mistake, that I was supposed to appear that afternoon, so I was taken back to County

Jail where I met other friends of mine. Well, me and my friends (not from Soledad) went to court that afternoon, when we returned, we happened to hear the news on the radio where it announced the killing of three inmates at Soledad Institution while scuffling in the yard. Damn, for some reason I knew what yard that man on the radio was referring to, because I fell to my knees against my will, and tears rolled out of my eyes. Believe me, I'm a man in every respect, but if you felt the tension we live under, you could easily understand a grown man crying. I was sad, glad, angry, and hateful; Gordon (a Black) also cried and he wasn't even at Soledad and yet we know how it is for Blacks in prison. Everybody stopped and stared at me not understanding. I cursed people out for no reason because, after all, it wasn't their fault. I returned here the next day and I could smell death in the air. The tier was like a tomb—I was put in my used to be, personal friend's cell; W. L. Nolen. I asked what happened and they told me (Blacks) that W. L. Nolen, Cleveland Edwards and Alvin Miller were shot down like ducks in a pond. Pay full attention to what I have said, because even today we live under the same conditions and that murder out in the yard could have easily been me or the rest of the Blacks down here. Or maybe we get it next time? All I do is ask myself, "It this the price a man has to pay for wanting to be Black and respected as such, as he respects others?" I tell you, it is cold blooded!

I speak in behalf of all Blacks who know and understand the meaning of being Black and in Prison. If it wasn't for those killings of W. L. Nolen, Edwards, and Miller, I would have never sat down to write this, but if my people keep on getting killed in this fashion, what is the sense in me living when their heart is also my beat?!

Cordially,
Hugo A. Pinell
A-88401 0-147

Witnessed by,
Thomas Lopez Meneweather
A-84502

STATEMENT OF FACTS

That: On the morning of January 13, 1970, (Tuesday) all of the inmates housed on the first floor of O-Wing, (a Maximum Security Section of the prison) at the California Correctional Training Facility at Soledad California, the floor informed all the inmates of Max-Row that the Max-Row yard was opening and more or less challenged everyone to go to the yard;

RELEASING PROCEDURE

That: Each inmate was released from his cell and instructed to proceed to a caged in area known as the sally port where our clothes were removed and handed to a guard who searched them then performed a skin shake which consists of checking the body orifices, after this we were allowed to dress and pass through the door to the Max-Row yard;

WHAT OCCURRED ON THE YARD

That: After being processed through the releasing procedures I passed through the door and entered the Max-Row yard; as I entered the yard I automatically looked up to the gun tower and found myself looking into the muzzle of a gun pointed at me, the tower guard then ordered me to go to the far end of the yard to the area of the hand ball court as he had so ordered each of the black inmates released to the yard prior to the time that I was released. After arriving at the hand ball court and exchanging greetings with my friends I played a game of hand ball with a friend; following the game of hand ball I went to a punching bag located in the area of the showers and punched the bag and I turned to face the opposite direction and watch another inmate punch the other bag down near the hand ball court. Just as I was turning back to face the gun tower inmate Nolen and another inmate started fighting and a shot rang out and inmate Nolen fell. I automatically started to him to find out if he was seriously hurt and to protect him from being attacked but as I glanced to my left I saw two Caucasian inmates running toward me and I shifted my body in order to meet the attack and repel it. Simultaneously, I saw inmate Cleveland Edwards rush toward inmate Nolen to see if he were seriously hurt and to protect him against an attack but then another shot was fired and his hands went to his stomach and he fell on his face. I swiftly knocked down the first of my attackers and shifted my position to meet his companion which put the one knocked down to my back and as I fought his companion inmate Alvin Miller yelled to me to watch my back, then he rushed to intercept the inmate at my back who was getting up. Just as he stepped between me and the gun tower another shot was fired and inmate Miller's hands went to his chest and he fell. By this time my second attacker was knocked down and I reversed my position to see if inmate Miller was OK, as I turned another shot was fired and blood started squirting from my left hand and I backed to the wall near the shower stall and the guard fired again and a Caucasian inmate slumped to the ground that I had been fighting with. He was behind me before I started backing to the shower wall. I looked at the tower guard and he was aiming the gun toward the wall near me and I thought then that he meant to kill me too so I moved from the wall as he fired and went over to stand over inmate Miller. All the time looking the guard in the gun tower in the face. He aimed the gun at me again and I just froze and waited for him to fire but he held his fire. After I saw he was not going to fire I pointed to where inmate Miller lay with two other black inmates bending over him and started to walk to him very slowly. The inmate I had played hand ball with suggested that I take inmate Miller to the hospital so I kneeled so inmate Miller could be placed on my shoulder then started to walk toward the door through which we had entered the yard and the tower guard pointed the gun at me and shook his head. I stopped and begged him for approximately ten minutes to let me take Miller to the hospital but all he did was shake his head. Then I started forward with tears in my eyes expecting to be shot down every second but the tower guard told Me "that's far enough" but then another guard gave me permission to bring Miller off the yard and I was ordered to lay him on the floor in the officers area and go to my cell which I refused to do until Miller was taken to the hospital. . . .

Thomas Lopez Meneweather

Soledad Central, California
Friday April 10, of 1970

Dear Sir;

1. I believe that I mentioned in my last letter that I have been confined here on the first floor of O-Wing (Max Row) since April of 1968. Shortly after my arrival a black inmate I had previously met at San Quentin whose name was Clarence Causey (nicknamed Dopey Dan) was assigned to a exercise group of six caucasian and mexican racist (anti black) inmates by himself and immediately he was set upon and viciously and wantonly stabbed to death by three of those inmates while prison guards stood indifferently by and watched the assault until Causey fell in a puddle of his own blood. Then they made the inmates in question back up and took inmate Causey's body off the tier and after repeated inquiries we the blacks was informed that inmate Causey was dead. And to make matters worse these same prison officials went to those inmate's trials and the end results was that Causey was accused of attacking them with a damn ink pen and they over powered him and took it away and killed him with it!!! Now, O-Wing is isolated and there is no inmate traffic from which knives can be smuggled into O-Wing without being detected by prison officials, nor do the O-Wing inmates have access to any metals with which to make knives plus security checks are made on an average of three times a month but still every non black inmate has virtually a collection of knives. Well anyway the following day after Causey was murdered some black inmates were able to purchase a knife from a Caucasian inmate who was having trouble with his own ethnic group and a Caucasian inmate

was stabbed in retaliation for the murder of Causey. At this point the exercise periods was segregated with respect to keeping blacks from exercising with non blacks.

2. Following this murder, another black inmate whose last name was Powell refused to come out of his cell and prison guards loaded about five different kinds of tear gas in his cell until he passed out then brought him out front to the officer's area and set upon him with gas guns, flash lights and clubs, this was witnessed by two inmates whose names and number I have plus the rest of us heard the commotions and the screams of Powell. He was taken to the prison hospital and we were informed by the prison officials that he was dead but his death was listed as Attributed to Heart Failure! We tried to bring this to the attention of the N.A.A.C.P., but as you can imagine our attempts were suppressed by the officials here and at that point never more than six blacks were allowed on Max Row which housed twenty-four inmates who race talk us in shifts so that it's done twenty-four hours a day, on their exercise periods they spit, throw urine and feces in our cells while the officials stand by in indifference and approval, they the officials calls us Hammers and Niggers too (both expressions means the same thing). The Prison Officials here stopped serving the meals and deliberately selected the Caucasian and Mexican inmates (described throughout this letter), to serve the meals and they immediately proceeded to poison our meals by filling food to be issued to us, with cleanser powder, crushed up glass, spit, urine and feces while the officials stood by and laughed, we rebelled by throwing these trays of contaminated food on the officials and on the tier, disciplinary reports were made against us and punishments imposed, but eventually they established a system where a black was assigned as half day porter (to serve meals and clean the tier) and one of the Caucasian or anti black Mexican inmates were assigned as porter for the remaining half day. This system eliminated their putting the above listed substances in our food since they did not want their food to receive the same or similar treatment by the black porter but they continued to throw these sub-

stances in our cells on us and our properties and race talk us as I stated above. Since my arrival here every black inmate that I'm acquainted with or has either heard of that is especially hated by officials at the various institutions, suspected of being involved in racial violence, or who is incarcerated for violence against police officers are systematically transferred here to Soledad and set up to be murdered by anti black inmates in the same or identical manner in which Clarence Causey was murdered, or run the risk of being rail roaded to death row by a corrupt and racist judicial system such as we are subjected to here in this Country, for self defense against the deliberate and consolidated efforts of prison officials and anti black prisoners to perpetrate genocide against us. The Solidarity of anti black prisoners and the officials here at Soledad is a open, common and accepted thing. Through experiences and by witnessing stabbings of black prisoners in the form and manner that deprived Clarence Causey of his life has made it abundantly clear to all of us that the Constitution and none of its rights are available to us and that further we are under siege in a race war, and we are determined that the price of our lives is the death of those who seek to murder us, for we owe our human rights to no one.

I declare under the penalty of perjury that the foregoing is true and correct.

Respectfully Submitted
Mr. Thomas Lopez Meneweather

After prison authorities learned that Meneweather had written his description of the January 13 shootings to attorneys, two whites filed the following affidavit, written under penalty of perjury.

On July 10, 1970 Mike and myself were taken from our cells here on the third tier by officer M. and two other officers whose names I don't remember, and were taken down stairs to the committee room where lieutenant E. and Mr. K. were waiting.

Upon entering the room Mr. K., Lt. E., and Officer M. told us to sit down, then they asked us in these words "do you know a goddam nigger name of Meneweather on max-row?" After we said no they began to tell us how they hated colored people and how they hated Meneweather especially because he was causing trouble for the staff by filing writs on them, and was snitching on Officer M. for killing those niggers on the yard to those no good nigger loving communist bastards trying to stir up trouble for the institution.

Then they said that they knew that we could influence the white guys on the second floor and then they told us that Meneweather is in jail for violence against a white man, and that he was also in the adjustment center now for another killing of a white dude up at San Quentin, and that he only had three years and a few months left before his discharge and that they didn't feel he had any right to live. Then they told us that they would see that Meneweather came upstairs about five days from then, and they said they would make it worth our while if we saw to it that Meneweather didn't live long enough to get off the second tier.

They told us if we didn't go through with it they would send me to Folsom or San Quentin and that the niggers are out to kill all the white dudes that were at Soledad Central and who were in O-Wing when the shooting happened in January. They said if we could catch him (Meneweather) off guard and kill him they would be sure to see to it that nobody went to court for it and that we would be protected for three or four months and then transferred to C.M.C. East, Camp or Palm Hall and get paroled in a year:

Carl James Tsouras

After being assaulted and beaten by ten guards at Soledad, a prisoner whose name is withheld by request was carried to an isolation strip cell.

I was at this time placed faced down and then the ever sadistic Sergeant M. for no legal nor normal reason started tearing my clothes off until I was naked and then turned me over on my back and started looking at my exposed organs with a look of pure sadistic pleasure on his face, he does this to every inmate that is moved from a cell or from one part of O-Wing to another by force.

Soledad
August 21, 1970

Dear Fay:

Blacks on Max Row have fallen under a darker cloud. Fay, no human being deserves the treatment we receive. You must help us by pushing the staff to completely segregate us from non-Black inmates. twenty-four (24) hours of psychological torture is enough to disturb the strongest mind—but our case is not so much that—as it is the need to better ourselves and we can't very well do so since there is no academical program and we haven't the money to purchase constructive material. And concentration is no longer a "power of mind" thing, it's almost an impossibility!

L.D. is back in isolation and I don't know if he has addressed you as yet, but that brother (L.D.) is not sick or crazy. He is tired, depressed, aware of the police harassment towards his person and thus, he reacts in a self-defense manner, but yet showing he really doesn't project violence or hate against these officials by merely throwing liquid or some powder in return for their unkindness. He is really relaying this message "officials drive us to the point of belief that our only meanings of protection is strictly on our own hands if we aim to survive." Other words, these staff members don't show us cooperation, respect—they don't show us anything but the fact that they aim to destroy us either physically or mentally!! There is no fear involved in our behavior—then again, there is no violence in our behavior! But my question is, what good does it do to withstand all these injustices if we remain in the same dungeon day after day? We are cautious! We are well behaved and yet nothing is granted. We simply don't want to remain down here anymore.

Today, some people from the main line came around gifting ice-creams to every inmate down here! Plus they brought a photographer to take pictures while the ice-cream was being dished-out! Can you see the picture? That has never been done before in the history of Max Row since I've been aware of this tier which goes back to 1965. I want you to know we didn't ask or wanted any ice-cream or any of their photographs and that we understand why it was done and that it was against our consent . . .

Respectfully,
Hugo A. Pinell
Max Row

Central Soledad
Sept. 24, 1970

Dear Miss Stender:

First of all, I want to thank you very much for the navigational text. I find it enlightening and giving a comprehensive conception of the science of Navigation. I will now be better prepared to enter a navigation school once released from prison.

From an outward appearance Soledad O-Wing has appeared to have changed. But underneath it is still as deadly for blacks as it ever was. The evil and sinister forces are still lurking in the shadows waiting for the spot-light of publicity to move to other locations. This was made manifest today (9-24-70) when one of the institution's maintenance personnel happened to stumble over a 13″ or 14″ inch long (mainline-made knife) when he came in to find out why the cell doors were not closing properly. After finding this one knife the Security Squad (goon squad, to us) was called in and three other foot long main line made shanks (knives) was also found hidden in the cell doors.

With the security that is practice in this wing, Black People can only resolve that some anti black guard let or brought these mainline made shanks into O-Wing. On Monday (9-21-70) the Goon Squad came in and searched the same tier that these four foot-long shanks were found on. We wonder why they didn't find them? Normally when weapons are found the institution takes pictures of them as they found them. We wonder why no pictures were taken of these four foot-long shanks which would confirm Black People's charges, along with the Black Caucus and Attorneys' charges, of institutional conspiracy against the welfare of Black inmates or anybody that they want removed.

We know that Black Parents, wives, friends and concerned citizens would like to know how these four, foot-long shanks, got into this maximum security building where every (speaking of Blacks *for sure*) inmate is shaken down before he leaves out and upon his return. Also two of these knives were found in the cell doors (on top the part where the doors slide back and forth) of occupied cells (two chicanos) and the other two were above unoccupied cells. We know that or deeply believe that had these weapons been above Black cells the authorities would not have hesitated in filing on Blacks or at least writing us up. None of these things so far has happened to the inmates involved. And we do not want this to happen. I am just letting you see the difference in treatment here at Soledad.

We now see and understand that the only way O-Wing will be safe for Black inmates is complete separation of the two races or various races. One on one side and the other on the other side of this building.

It is no doubt in our minds who these shanks were intended for if ever trouble broke out. Black people are kept in such a tight security watch that they are lucky to get a razor blade, not to think of four foot-long shanks made and grinded to razor sharpness on the mainline. These are the questions now in the minds of Black inmates here in seemingly peaceful Soledad O-Wing.

Thank you again for your concern and trouble
Sincerely Your Client
(Name withheld by request)

Soledad
September 14, 1970

Dear Sister:

Today is the 14th of September; tomorrow, the 15, I will be released onto the exercise tier with an inmate who just three days ago was hurling human feces and urine at me and other Brothers here on Max Row. The above move is an attempt by *Prison officials* to force integration on a group of whites who have avowed to "exterminate Niggers," or otherwise harm Blacks upon opportunity.

I am to proceed to the tier with the said prisoner, even though I'm with the knowledge that officials have armed the said inmate, in an effort to perpetrate my death. Yet, in this matter I am prepared to accept whatever fate is ahead.

I have faith in my ability to defend myself. And I shall do so fully. Nevertheless, if an altercation takes place, prison officials will surely trump charges against me, if I am the victor. A belief that I predicate upon the historical profile of the prison, related to incidents in the past of a like kind and where blacks have been made to suffer trumped up charges for being victorious in the situations.

My purpose for writing is in that whatever the termination, may the ultimate end reflect the truth

All power to the People!

Earl L. Satcher

Soledad
October 10, 1970

Dear Sister:

At present I am confined in the "Isolation" section of the Prison. Such is the condition pursuant to the following:

October the 5th, Mr. Flowers was removed by prison officials to a section of the prison known as "X Wing." This change resulted in "Max Row" being populated with one Black (me) and four whites.

The morning of the 5 Oct 70, Officer H. approached my cell and asked, "Satcher you want to be the porter with inmate A?" I replied, "If you unlock my cell, I have no alternative but to walk onto the tier." Officer H. unlocked the cell.

Inmate A and myself walked onto the tier when the "bar" was thrown. And though the element was at first tense, we managed to accomplish getting the porter duties done. And as the day drew to an end, the disappointment that an incident hadn't taken place was apparent on the faces and in the attitudes of the prison guards.

The following morning of the 6th Inmate "A" and myself were busy with the porter duties. When the Program Administrator for "O Wing" ventured in. He came onto "Max Row" and talk about yard privileges. He then suddenly called to Officer H. to turn the Bar to key position. Whereas he promptly proceeded to unlock the cells of inmates b, c, and d, all of which are white and with whom I've had severe conflicts within the past while on Max Row. At this happening, the program Administrator left the tier and locked the Sally port gate, leaving five prisoners on the tier one Black (myself) and prisoners A, B, C, and D. (In other sections of the prison integrated exercises are conducted in an equal number basis of each race.)

Inmate "B" approached me with inmate "C," a towel in one hand and a domino box in the other. The following transpired:

Inmt. B: "You play dominos man?"

Earl: "Yea, what you got in mind?"

Inmt. B: "Nothing but a domino game."

Earl: "Fine, squat on the tier and lets play."

At this point inmate d joins the group, sits directly in front of me to play opposite as a partner. The dominos are scattered face down and we all draw seven each.

Inmt. B to C: "You going to fall your hand?" "No," replies Inmate C. "Then I guess it's on d," Inmate B continues. "What you going to do d?' A replies in answer, "I ain't doing no good, my hand is dead." Inmate C cuts in, "The count so far is *headup*."

["Headup" in prison refers to any fight between two prisoners on the agreement that the friends of either of the two fighters will not interfere with the fight.]

Inmt. B to Earl: "Where you at?"

Earl to B: "You all are calling the shots, I'm playing dominos — I suggest that if the pig won't let us to the yard for sunshine and exercise, we should together get the pig to extend the exercise period from one hour to two, or maybe all day."

Inmate B to Earl: "Yes, that's a good idea."

We all then played two games of dominos and drink coffee which in all lasted about 45 minutes. Until officer H. ordered a return to cells. But it was apparent that the guards were stunned!

Oct. 7, 1970. After inmate A and myself finished serving the noon meal officer H. ventured to the tier and announced for every inmate to pack his personal property as "Max Row" was being disbanded; he further informed me that I was scheduled to move to "X Wing" 1st floor. At learning this news I questioned officer H. as to why "X Wing" and he replied so as for other inmates to hear, "Damn, Satcher, we've tried and tried to get you off Max Row. Now we are sending you to X Wing, we want you under the gun." (Meaning the gun tower located in X Wing hall-way.) To this I replied, "I have no unarmed defense against bullets, therefore, I shall refuse any transfer to "X Wing," either move me upstairs in this same building ("O Wing") or just send me to the hole and let me be in peace." Thus, I'm here in isolation, the "hole," and have been told I shall be here until I agree to the X Wing transfer, which I won't do. But after 29 days (the legal maximum time one may be kept on isolation) more than likely the guards will attempt to force the transfer, but I shall fight any such attempt for all I'm worth. ("In any defense the objective is to preserve oneself, at the same time defense becomes supplement to attack," Mao.)

I went before the disciplinary Committee on charges of refusing an order to transfer. I requested to be transferred to the Chino Adjustment Center. The request was denied, and again I was told, this time by the Program Administrator that, "We want you under the Gun, Satcher."

While here in the hole, I've met and talked with a prisoner (white) who apparently needs help. He seems to be a victim of the intricate web of eradication woven by prison officials. He was sort of kicked out of the "Nazi clique" here at Soledad because of his association with Blacks, as I understand it . . .

Here I draw my letter to an end. I believe I'm pushing on borrowed time, but I'm still smiling, because I know my day will come.

My regards as always.

A brother in arms and truth
Earl
(Earl Satcher)

Soledad
October 19, 1970

Dear Sister,

. . . this X Wing environment is filled with profound tension as a result of a fight which occurred Friday between Black and White inmates in X Wing exercise yard.

The rumor is that certain white inmates plan to retaliate, and progress from fist fighting to weapons. This weekend I have been trying to cool things down, but officer M. has been working this wing for two days, and the Black inmates are extra paranoid, because we all know his reputation as a racist officer. I explain to the Brothers that the officials sent officer M. in here as a psychological thing to cool the Brothers down, but the Brothers are still cynical toward officer M.

I am doing my best to alleviate the situation here, but here's two inmates who were on Max Row with Randolf, Eugene, myself, and other Black inmates, and these two came over here and started fighting with Black inmates from the very beginning; in fact, the fight Friday stemmed from one of these particular inmates doing something to one of the Black inmates in the past, then coming over here and boasting about it, and singing that Nigger song he invented on Max Row.

Sister in all honesty we are sincerely tired of getting into these fights, which only prolong our stay in prison, but one must protect himself.

As you know we don't have access to weapons, so that why we try to stay in top physical shape, and learn to use our hands and feet.

Power to all oppressed People!

Sincerely your,

Madison Flowers, Jr.

November 1, 1970

AFFIDAVIT OF DEPOSITION OF DEMANDS

To whom it may concern "with emphasis on all prison personnel (locally and otherwise) and the general public."

We the inmate-prisoners of "O-Wing" here at Soledad Central, interracially, individually and collectively and in the same terms as ethnic groups, Black, Brown and Caucasian, and after years of racial conflict, wish to officially and formally serve notice on you that no longer will we allow you to manipulate us and exploit our mutual suffering from the conditions imposed on us by your individual and concerted efforts to dehumanize us and perpetrate against us every crime conceivable to your distorted minds for your sadistic satisfactions. You have maliciously, sadistically and premeditatedly reduced living conditions within the confines of these human cesspools of mental suffering and physical abuse that you choose to call institutions and training facilities to reduce our very daily existence to anguish, frustration, anxieties and despair and then set us one upon and against the other(s), subject only to the restrictions of your whims and tastes, "individually and concertedly." This irresponsible, irrational and inhumane behavior on your parts has resulted in the deaths of various inmates and serious bodily and mental injury to many others and the time, even though much overdue, has come that these acts on your part will no longer be tolerated and by whatever means necessary will we struggle to effect the destruction of havens of lies and general propagandering and deceit of the public to freely practice these unlawful and inhumane acts against us. In addition, we submit the following list of grievances and demands in an effort to better the lives and living conditions of all inmate-prisoners concerned. You are further officially and formally advised and informed that we will go and remain on a hunger strike until our demands are reasonably and satisfactorily met:

1. Abolish the rule and practice of removing inmates from the main line on the whims of individual or various officials who "suspect" the inmate of violating an institutional rule, or of having committed a public offense and thus without any concrete evidence of the inmate's guilt warehousing him in isolation, max-rows, segregations or A/C for indeterminate periods of time.

2. That the section in institutional rules with regard to mail and visiting privileges wherein it requires that an incarcerated person (inmate-prisoner) is prohibited from corresponding and visiting with anyone he didn't know for at least six months personally prior to his incarceration be repealed and abolished in as it serves to and is designed to limit and for some inmates preclude altogether contact with free society.

3. That all inmate-prisoners under indictment or being tried by information or preliminary examination for the commission of a public offense while incarcerated be it a capital offense or otherwise, and who has been subjected to restricted visiting privileges because of these pending charges be allowed at least a minimum of three hour visits and thereafter to visit all day or until another inmate similarly situated receives a visit and cannot visit unless he has access to that particular area in use. This demand is designed with the Soledad Seven in mind and to insure that they will be given a reasonable time to visit with their family, friends and loved ones who have traveled from far away places like Los Angeles, California.

4. That a wider variety of foods be made available to the in-

mates of O and X wings, such as fried eggs, hot cereals, meats, "beef, lamb, fish, chicken, etc.," because there are many inmates who don't eat pork for health and religious reasons respectively, also that the noon meal be restored in the place of the sandwiches if we cannot be given a wider variety to choose from. Peanut butter, dog food tuna and bologna for seven days a week and three hundred and sixty-five days a year after year is unreasonable and this has been the noon meal for more than two years.

5. Abolish the so-called special isolation diet because it is unedible, unclean and endangers the health of inmates restricted to it. Further, reinstate the policy of giving desirable foods left over from the meals to the porters. Also, since second helpings of food is not allowed us, put a larger amount on the trays because eighty per cent of the prisoners here do not get enough to eat on their trays at each meal.

6. Abolish the system of warehousing inmates by placing them in the A/C or segregation center for various lengths of times and in some cases indefinitely and then when forced to transfer them by public concern, you always send them to the A/C or segregation section of another prison to begin the ordeal all over again.

7. That inmate, Raymond Alvarez, be immediately placed on the main line since he has no problems of adjustment nor has he proven himself to be a disciplinary problem. He has further been under indefinite commitment to O-Wing since 1967.

8. Repeal Rule D1201 of the rules of the director of the California Department of Corrections on the grounds that it is too vague and limited for the powers it confers on prison officials in terms of "inmate behavior" that warrants disciplinary action. This rule further allows prison officials to assume the duties and powers of a legal court of law without affording the accused inmate any of the procedural and constitutional rights and privileges otherwise enjoyed by persons in a legal court of law; i.e. right to confront accuser; present evidence in defense; right to legal counsel, etc. This is especially emphasized when inmates are accused or suspected of having committed a public offense while

serving time in the various prisons of the California Penal system. In each case the prison officials arrest prisoners suspected of committing a public offense, places him in isolation and thereafter tries convicts and punishes him for commission of the public offense, without any of the rights mentioned supra being adhered to "all under D1201" and thereafter refers it to the office of the public prosecutor, who in fact is the only power with legal jurisdiction in the matter in the first place.

9. Repeal and abolish the practice of subjecting prisoners to double punishment for infraction of prison rules, by subjecting prisoners of being tried, convicted and punished for alleged infractions of prison rules D 1201: then placing the same write-up in the inmates central file to be reviewed by the California Adult Authority, who has the responsibility of determining how much time each man is to spend incarcerated because the board reads the write-up, the finding of the prison officials and then decides the fate of the prisoner solely on these write-ups, thus subjecting him to a double trial and punishment which in the latter respect is a denial of parole for periods ranging from six months up to three or more years.

10. That the human rights commission look into and file a petition on the behalf of Angela Davis in the United States Supreme Court (in Washington, D.C.) to determine the issue as to whether or not prisoners housed in city or state correctional facilities pending disposition of alleged public offenses brought against them are being denied due process and equal protection of law by the officials of these respective institutions and facilities by their subjecting the accused to arbitrary punishments such as denying them the same privileges enjoyed by persons (prisoners) similarly situated solely on the basis that they are charged with the commission of a public offense, which amounts to the prison officials in question assuming the powers and duties of a legal court of law and thereafter trying, convicting and punishing the accused person without affording him the constitutional rights and safeguards otherwise enjoyed in a legal court of law.

11. That Earl Satcher, who is confined in the isolation section

of O-Wing be adjusted on upper O-wing with fellow inmates whom he is properly able to function with, rather than be transferred to X-wing, where he doesn't feel comfortable or secure. No inmate should be forced against his will.

Soledad
Nov. 13, 1970

Sister Fay:

Today, Friday November 13, 1970 is a day I will long remember, our hunger strike has ended, two weeks of self inflicted punishment, all of which was in vain. All we actually won with the exception of Mr. Alvarez at last leaving here, was soup at lunch time—at least this is the only immediately visible gain. Many here including myself have never participated in any form of meaningful protest before, perhaps we expected too much. . . .

Things here are not well, something will take place in order for everyone to work off the frustration of this mass disappointment. Two weeks we hungered, to be told that it is and will always be departmental policy for us to be treated as things or caged animals always subject to the whims and caprices of our arbitrary keepers. In their estimation to be imprisoned in this state is to become non-human, with subsequent loss of all constitutional guarantees.

Sincerely Yours
Leroy Nolan Fleming

P.S. I have not lost hope or faith, today soup; tomorrow the world.

Soledad
Dec. 18, 1970

Dear Fay;

Outwardly and materially our food strike was a dismal failure, we only gained a bowl of soup, but the harmony, unity, and greater understanding that evolved between the races was a tremendous gain, but immediately after the strike, the staff no longer held inmate staff meetings, certain porter positions and privileges were eliminated and the rumors of pending racial clashes began to fly from certain keepers mouths. Fay, you must live this to fully understand. Here is a man who consciously or not, hates a class of people, he is also a racist, he is paid a salary and made to feel important, for being a keeper, he has eight hours of duty which is non-productive, therefore boring, he answers to no one other than others of his ilk and mentality, and in cages before him lie those he considers a threat to his values. He plays a crude Pavlovian game with his victims to pass his time and if we don't react as he would like, if we cling to manliness, what fury he feels, what hate. Murder, human destruction is his next move.

You have in your last letter, accused me of being too optimistic concerning what tomorrow will bring, my dream of a better society. Fay, that dream is all that allows me to retain my humanity, it is my hold on sanity. If I for one moment accepted as reality, as final, my position, the oppression of my people, if I submitted to the classism, racism, and anti-life forces and ceased to dream, ceased to plot another course, what reason would I have for living, how constructive could my thoughts and actions remain? I dream a big dream, keep the impossible as my immediate goal, but I also try to take realistic steps. Fay, I was born a slave, a slave because of many things, color not being the only chains, many of all colors and greeds share the conditions of my birth, many share the life and conditions of valueless existence, and many of us share the same desire that no price is too high to break those shackles, all of us at one time or another will be called upon to make big sacrifices so that others will have new values and goals, heroes to emulate. To provide me and others with dignity, many have sacrificed and one day we must do the same, our only restriction is to insure that we pay in a manner that is not empty and meaningless.

                                                    Always,
                                                    Nolan

Soledad
February 5, 1971

Fay Stender:

You may recall who I am but this can only be by the letters I wrote you, a while back, in request of urgent assistance on behalf of brothers receiving foul treatment. And yes again, I'm writing in request of your assistance for the brothers that are being accused of the incident that occurred here in O-Wing East Block, Feb. 1, 1971 supposedly stabbing of 2 guards. Ha! Leroy Fleming A-91028, Edward Whiteside A-91150, Raymond Marquez B-22318, *are not accused,* according to this pig-pen system, they *are guilty* and being treated in beyond such a manner!! The truth belongs to the people and what is befalling them is purely inhuman! They have been made a separate part of the prison. Beyond strip-cell treatment: They were thrown into separate cells, without *any* bedding, pure steel and concrete block naked and with orders that they were to receive nothing. A guard on second watch, not knowing what the 'new, inhuman, procedure was, by pure human morals gave them limited clothing and simple bedding and as far as we know, might now be fired or assigned to the towers. They are not allowed any thing other than what they got, no materials as paper envelopes nor even a pencil! Fleming, Marquez and Whiteside, received visits immediately after the 1st., and were only allowed a *half* hour to visit and hand cuffed from the cell to and while visiting. They were not even given the chance to shower in order to try to wash away some of the *gas* they were sprayed with that still affects them as of today. Also, Marquez was still suffering the effects of the beating he received in his cell on the 31st. of Jan. When questioned of his determination in testifying for Brother Yogi answering positively on his behalf, he was then given such a beating and further: Not given any proper medical treatment nor a chance to go see the doctor. In regards to the food; they have told the guard that there is an irregular taste in the food which is not as the same food given elsewhere in O-Wing. With no response given them, they refrained from chancing such food and resorted to whatever food their brother convicts can sneak them. If they are accused of some offense then they should be processed as the procedure goes. They request to go to isolation or the strip-cells. And above all the opportunity to contact their attorneys. Their only reply is an indifferent attitude and further foul treatment under the pretense of investigation. In urgent need they request your assistance. Come witness yourself and be sure that many stand ready and willing to bring such facts before you. Bring an assistant and whatever more help you are certain may alleviate their unjustice.

Come as immediately as possible and with the request to observe yourself the housing condition they are forced to endure. I'm nearly positive as to your response to *our* request Fay. I remember your reaction to Bobby Soto's request. In prediction, I thank you Fay. Hope your presence is immediate if no sooner.

Joe

Soledad
Sunday Feb. 7, 1971

Dear Fay;

I am at this moment quite upset, and if the truth be known, somewhat apprehensive, since I am in a word, entangled in a situation of unknown proportions, not of my making, beyond my controlled comprehension, just like a lamb, I await the slaughter, Let me run down what is at this moment happening and then perhaps you can at least sense, the immense pressure that I labor under. The third tier had been vacated for over two months, with the incident, all three of us have been placed up here, alone, no exercise, no fraternity with peers, no property, I am a man with immense pride, but I'm forced to beg others with resources no greater than I, to wait upon the whims and caprices of all that challenge my codes to take care of all that should be a matter of course, I hate with a passion to kow tow, kiss ass and strain up with people, just to seek allies, that may not be sincere. This third tier is not pure isolation, we are with shouting range of all the A.C. programmers on this side but there the comparison ends, none of us have been allowed exercise, or showers, my property legal or otherwise have been systematically denied so in a sense this third tier is but a slick isolation. The title which they use to justify my move is that of Administrative Segregation; just one slick term used to fuck over any and all, they in their distorted thinking use any title to justify whatever their whims dictate, and I, sucker that I am, cannot challenge them. They are Gods, beholden to no one, so in the final ayalysis, I must eventually break, but when and how and to achieve what purpose should be foremost is dim. The officer that was allegedly attacked is back on duty at the same station, is handling our food, what thoughts must be running through his mind.

Today, they allowed one of us at a time on the tier for showers, when my time came I made it quite clear that to get me back in my cage, more than a request would be needed to get me back in my house or cell, don't mistake me, I know that if they presented a united front, I would be forced to succumb to superior odds, but my ethics, my grasp on right and wrong, my being fed up with tokenism, my need to reassert my manhood whatever that may be pushed me to take the so called foolish stand, but Fay, foolish or not it was me; I was prepared to have my head resemble a watermelon, but I knew I was right, I wanted was for one piggish fool to be the first, after that I would not have given a damn on the consequences, all I wanted was to vent my frustration upon just one, anyone. For some reason they recognized that the cost might outweigh the hope for results. Whatever the reason, they submitted, moved me back to the second tier, old cell, my only restriction is that I am on cell exercise pending the disciplinary on a write up "115" that has yet to be submitted or written, but at least I am once again protected by the committed for real group, so I feel more comfortable in mind if not physical. They may never take me to the committee, but fuck it, I know what the scheme was and knowledge adds to my strength.

Fay, do not attempt to bag me, I still suffer from a hang up called trying to get back—I don't believe that sincerity nor purpose are of any importance other than preparing and changing for eventual release. Broadway is, was and will always be my goal, take that from and I am lost. Many things I have done and will continue to do are only done because of pride and the emotional response of the moment, beyond my control. Taking this into consideration, one may be tempted to call me a coward, an escapist and a punk, but I for all my tender years know that to commit an act, however noble but without adequate safeguard is but suicide, and I am not looking for that, to die is easy, to live is the hassle, to live with purpose and meaning. I am not condemning, all of us must at one time or another martyr themselves. But Fay, if I ever get caught up in the big move, you will not have to bite your nails, fearing a call from me. If I move, I in front know what my chances of survival are and if negative, I will be prepared to go for broke alone. I am not building you, to me you are just another bitch, who happens to know law, as such, I cannot depend upon you, will not depend. But by the same token, help can never be denied, what I'm trying to say is that all three of these funny beefs I have picked up in the last seven months, are not mine, call them frames, conspiracies or any slick title, but my motives for trying to inform you has been because of my love of my brothers and that the evidence has been superficial or non existent. This latest episode is a pure frame, beyond my control. It is not necessary for you to believe, but the truth can never be distorted. We will not debate your degree of commitment, to a degree I have to trust you, all I want you to recognize is that I Nolan Fleming would not waste your time, that could be better spent with my comrades, if I was not suffering grave injustice. This is not to infer that you should drop everything to see about me, but to make you aware that for many reasons I have been placed on a list for extermination. I write this in anger, I have no other outlets for my unbridled anger and hate.

One last thing if possible, my constituents took the liberty to get in touch with my sister and Aunt, explaining my then predicament. You receive mail by the tons, all requiring some sort of overt action, so your time is not yours after all, but I must and will make a request. My sister and my Aunt have been strained up with me for over 17 years, if possible just send each of them a form letter, explaining how mistakes happen and of my presumed innocence, just a four line form letter will suffice, they have been on the line of cutting me loose so long, thoughts of any complicity on my part would and will push them over. There is nothing I could possibly say to salvage the harm, they have seen me go through far too many changes and like all squares they believe the law is always right. So Fay, I ask for you to run down all preceding events, from Jan. 1970 on my lack of involvement in any of it. If I was to lose them, life would be like quicksand. If you cannot do this, say so, but if your answer is to the affirmative, say it and mean it. My life is a contradiction to their values, but they love me, and it is of importance to me that they understand that this is more than cops and robbers, whatever, let me know. I look forward to our meeting now, more than ever. This makes the 3rd 115 and either must have them removed or rewritten to mirror fairness and truth.

I'm quite proud of your efforts for my less fortunate comrades may all turn out well.

One last word and I'll close, if you are unable to contact my kin for any reason, do not hesitate to say so.

May You Remain Firm And Committed.
Nolan

Soledad
February 20th, 1971

Dear Mrs. Stender:

This letter and its contents are addressed to you in good faith, and it's our sincere hope that the following will be used in any way or form to better the degrading and sadistic treatment that convicts Marquez and Whiteside are being handed by the Prison Regime, and their puppets and pawns.

On the 9th day of February, 1971, an incident took place involving Marquez and Whiteside upon their arrival on this side of O-Wing, wherefore an officer by the name of E. refused to issue both said convicts any mattresses to sleep on, blankets, sheets, toilet tissue, soap, and clothing of any kind. Both these men are under medication and when it was time for them to receive their medication, they did not get it, so both convicts started calling said officer for their medication—this sadistic dog boldly replied, "You two animals shut your ———— mouths, I'll give you your pills when I feel like it, you keep hollering and you could get more than just your pills." Both convicts told Officer E. to quit talking all that garbage, and bring the medication and that while he's at it to bring some mattresses, blankets, etc. Approximately thirty (30) minutes later, said officer finally went up and told Marquez, "About them mattresses and things, you can forget about getting them, you can also forget about and not bother to ask the night-officer to furnish you with a mattress or anything else, your lucky your getting your pills." Where upon said officer threw Marquez's medication on the floor, and said, "Get on your knees you dirty ———— chili-choker and pick up your drugs. Keep it in mind spick, you'll never make it out of prison alive, you and your nigger friend are going to pay for what you S.O.B.'s done." Marquez replied, "Get the ———— out of here Pig, you just give us our issue and go talk that trash to somebody that wants to hear it." Said officer did Likewise to Whiteside, threatened his life and called him a sack of dirty niggers.

These two men have not been eating any state food; that can and more than likely is tampered with—they just eat things that they can purchase from the canteen; for officers and some known queers are the ones that handle the food and the officers are the only ones allowed to serve these two men. It's a known fact that these puppets and pawns do not hesitate to spit and put uncouth things in the food . . . and one of the officials who was allegedly assaulted is here five (5) days a week, is one of the puppets making up the food-trays—a fatal chemical causing cancer or some other fatal disease could be put in these convicts food . . . one has to realize that we're dealing with some very scurvy dogs . . . need more be said?

On the 11th day of February, 1971, we went to the yard and when we came back the tier was smelling of tear-gas. Upon inquiring, we found out that Marquez and Whiteside were sadistically tear-gassed while in their cells, for since they've been on this side they have not been allowed to shower or exercise. On February 13, 1971, we went to the yard and when we came back, again Marquez and Whiteside were sadistically tear-gassed.

Marquez and Whiteside are not supposed to be on isolation-status, yet they are not allowed to have their property. Otis Paulo Tugwell, Carl James Tsouras, and myself and other convicts have tried to send books and magazines to Marquez and Whiteside; and the officers have refused to take anything to these two men. On the 12th day of February 1971, one officer by the name of H. threatened Tugwell, Tsouras and myself for wanting and requesting said officer to take some books to Marquez and Whiteside. Officer H. very calmly said to me, "I'm not taking a ————— thing to them two ————— punks and if you keep persisting with wanting to make life easier for those two creeps, you'll also be there with them getting the same treatment, perhaps even worse for sympathizing with them ————— holes." This was right after he passed out mail that he threatened me.

Marquez and Whiteside asked this same sadistic H. if he could give them mattresses and so forth (for this is his first time on this shift, 4:00 p.m. until 12:00). This puppet and punk said, "You two punks aren't getting nothing other than your medication until I get orders from my superiors, but until then you two S.O.B.'s will be treated like animals." At about 8:00 p.m. or so, myself and others smelled tear-gas and this sadistic officer H. was saying to Marquez and then to Whiteside, "You two ————— animals can sleep on that." The next day (13th of Feb., 1971) said officer gassed both convicts again.

On the 16th day of February, 1971, Marquez and Whiteside

were tear-gassed . . . On the 18th day of February, 1971 . . .
On the 19th day of February 1971; also Officer H. gassed both
men that night. Every time they gassed these men during the day
we were out on the yards; today the same thing; and just awhile
ago that little punk H. (it's 9:30 right now, so it must have been
about 9:00 p.m.) tear-gassed both Marquez and Whiteside, and
threatened their lives. All this sadistic harassment has got to
come to a halt immediately, these two men's life are in extreme
danger, get an injunction or something and have them removed
to some place a little safer.

We are willing to sign any legal document attesting to the
foregoing as true to the extent as to which each one of us knows,
and will take the stand in any court of law and testify against
the Prison Regime that they have willfully and sadistically broken
any constitutional protection guaranteed to these two convicts—
Marquez and Whiteside—as human beings.

Respectfully Yours,
Francisco Albarran Buelna

I certify and declare under the penalty of perjury that the foregoing is true and correct.
Dated this *20th* day of *February, 1971.*

*Earl Satcher was transferred to Folsom Prison from Soledad in
December, 1970. Attempts on his life did not end with that transfer, however.*

Folsom
February 18, 1971

Dear Mrs. Stender,

At present I'm incarcerated in the California State Prison of
Folsom at Represa, California. My housing unit within this same
prison is building number 4—or Adjustment Center.

Today at this location a here to be related incident occurred.
Because it involves a client of yours, I'm (at his request) relating

to you the details of this event.

Because of the seriousness of this incident I would prefer not to mention names in this correspondence.

The following is a copy of a memo made by me concerning the above mentioned. It is true and correct in every respect— only the names of the Staff members and inmates involved (beside myself) have been omitted.

Today while on my way to the Adjustment Center yard for the regular afternoon exercise period a building staff member stopped me and made the following remark or proposal.

Well I hear that you were put up for G.P. review? (recommended by Adjustment Center committee at 90 days review for general population housing consideration, on the morning of 18th February 1971).

I responded, Yes I was.

Staff member, do you expect to make it? (be approved).

My answer, No—not really.

Staff member, you don't like nigger black panthers, do you Benner?

No answer by me.

Staff member, Benner, when I call you back in from the yard today, I will bring you in (out of turn) with S., start a rumble, (fight) with him and you won't have any trouble getting approved for G.P. — Just start a rumble and then get out of the way, and things will start looking up for you around here—. You got that Benner?

I made no response.

Staff member, It's either that or trouble for you Benner!

After saying this the yard door was opened and I was allowed out. I made no other reply— Why? Partly out of shock, and to be honest—partly out of fear.

Once on the yard I located ————, whom I know only by sight and I proceeded to retell the remarks and or proposal made to me by the here above mentioned staff member, the inmate concerned gave me your name and address and requested that I relate to you this conversation and its proposal as made to me.

Becoming involved in something like this can only worsen my situation here (prison) and it will probably have long range effects on future parole consideration. But I have to do something —If I do not tell somebody then I remain vulnerable. The staff involved surely will not want me to repeat this proposal—and they must have noticed my talking to the inmate in question on the yard today, so I must assume that they suspect that I told the inmate everything.

While being called in from the yard—I was called out of turn, along with the inmate in question. But when I made no move to comply the staff member in question made a move that appeared to be a recheck of the list of persons, (and their order of return from the yard), and *then* correctly called the name of the person ordinarily scheduled to come in with ————.

I am scheduled to come in from the yard on the last group. When I did the staff member in question only response was to give me a glaring stare. Apparently he decided against any further comment because I was then accompanied by another inmate.

Below are a list of persons to whom I am sending letters concerning this matter—also included are carbon copies of those letters. I have no idea how else to proceed with this matter but I feel that it is extremely important that something be done to prevent any further future attempt on this person. I also feel it important to establish my position, including my total lack of participation on anything of this nature.

Because I wish to assist you in protecting the well-being of this person, (your client) I will *not* identify either his identity or the staff members identity until I have been assured by you that it is safe and wise to do so, I remain.

Very Truly Yours,
L. Wayne Benner

Copies enclosed;
Walter E. Craven, Warden Folsom Prison
Raymond Procunier, Director California Department of Corrections
His Honorable Judge DeCristoforo, Superior Court of Sacramento

Soledad
March 23, 1971

Dear Elaine:
Monday after you and the other attorneys left, myself and all the other inmates on my tier and others tiers were committed to unsanitary and cruel punishment. The toilets were turned off and we were not fed and today myself and Bobby Soto (March 23, 1971) had hot coffee thrown on us and were gassed. None of us were fed. None of us on O-1 have clothes except shorts and socks and we have no sheets. Something must be done to stop these people from threatening us this way. We wish that you and other attorneys would get some kind of court order against this type of treatment or investigate or something. We consider this quite an emergency. Also please see what can be done to have me removed from this tier like they told me they were going to do in committee or to the line or to another institution.

By the way when myself and Bobby Soto were gassed and had hot coffee thrown on us we were in our cells and did no kind of harm to the officer that did this or any of the other officers that are doing the same thing.

They've made no effort so far to give anyone on the tier clothes or anything to clean the hot coffee that was thrown on us out of our cell. There are 8 or 9 of us on this tier going through the treatment.

All we ask is to be treated like human beings which we are. We wish that something will be done as soon as possible. Thank you.

Yours Truly,
Ramon M. Shryock
B-28722 0-138

P.S. Regards from all the brothers.

Soledad
March 24, 1971

Dear Elaine:

More things are happening here left and right. Today (March 24, 1971) myself, Raymond Marquez, and Leonard Stance were forced by 21 officers on the tier with a gas gun in one hand and a club in the other, to clean the tier and there was some outside the gate with shotguns ready to fire. We had no choice but to come out our cells in shorts and shower thongs and clean the tier. And on the second tier C-Wing the inmates were dosed with gas and 3 shotguns brought in and one shotgun fired. Something must be done we need some support or get me away from here cause their layen dead to get certain inmates. I hope you and your associates will be able to do something for us as soon as possible before more inmates are hurt. Thank you. Regards from all the brothers.

Venceremos
Ramon M. Shryock

A prison guard was killed at Soledad in July of 1970. After an unusually long delay, seven black prisoners were charged with the murder. (Months later, the prosecution dismissed charges against four of the accused for lack of evidence.) Witnesses for the prosecution were transferred out of Soledad and kept in special confinement at Chino.

Chino
October 18, 1970

Dear Mrs. Stender:

Is is possible for you to send me the name and address of the attorney who is representing those seven inmates at Soledad who allegedly killed that cop at North?

The eight rats that are testifying against them are here on the first tier Westside. The State has offered them all paroles for testifying, and yesterday gave each of them $20.00 in canteen.

The one named B. and Tony said that they were testifying just so they could get the parole and that they didn't see who killed that cop. But since the officials said they would be released they are going to testify against them.

There is about ten people here who would be willing to testify to this. Also that for testifying they get special privileges and canteen that is paid for by the State.

I think this would come under bribery and be an issue at trial, because the State has used this special privilege to get them to testify. Some of them said unless they are released they wouldn't testify and once released would leave the State before trial. So this is self evident that they're willing to send those guys to the gas chamber just to obtain their release and not because they know anything.

Not only that but the state is paying them to testify. One of them named L. or L. said he is being paid $80.00 and will get more after the trial.

I am going to have every one here that heard it write it in an affidavit and sign it. I can send it (the affidavits) to you or who ever is the attorney for those guys.

The officials won't let us get around them and we have to talk from our cells. Otherwise we might encourage them to change their minds. But these guys are actually being paid by the state to testify, plus promised a release after they testify.

I would like to write to that attorney and tell him all this. Also one official who helped bribe these guys was Captain R. at North Facility. I knew him at San Quentin "66."

Very Sincerely Yours
Gary

Soledad
April 5, 1971

OPEN LETTER TO THE PRESS

Dear Sir:

Perhaps the public, yourself included, are tired of hearing of the many incidents that originate from this prison, but I assure you that no one can be tireder than we, the victims of this mad house. I would like to clarify your article of April 1, concerning using chemical agents in O-Wing, tear gas is much too humane a name for what was used. The men were gassed in their cells that night and gassed on the tier two days later, also shot-guns were brought into this wing to force them back into their cells. I will not attempt to explain what provoked these two incidents, to do so I would have to attempt to justify an insane situation to sane people. Let me just say that most men have been in O-Wing eight months or longer with two years not infrequent or unusual. Some ninety percent of the men in here are under psychiatric care, which only means they receive drugs with no therapy, all of this coupled with living in cages, some 22 hours a day, watched over by insensitive, authoritative personnel leads to incidents whose cause, only the fully initiated can understand or appreciate.

I have another incident that just occurred on this day, that I would like to relate if I may. James Wagner, Roosevelt Williams and myself Jesse Phillips have been charged since last July with the death of a guard in the North Facility. Friday, April 2, 1971 we were summoned one by one to the hospital and were asked to submit to a blood test by order of the District Attorney handling our case, we refused asking to be allowed to contact our attorneys to make sure that they were aware of this development and to gain their permission. This was deemed impossible and we in return informed the associate supt. S. that it would be in violation of our rights to take the test without informing at least one of our attorneys. We were taken back to the wing with the understanding that they would contact someone. Monday April 5, they came again with a piece of paper, they refused to let any of us read, which they claim was a court order ordering us to take the test. Once again we explained that we would submit to the test only after receiving verbal assurance from one of our attorneys, that it was legal. The blood test in this matter is an attempt to gather evidence and since we are all under indictment, scheduled for trial in thirty days and have attorneys, we felt that to allow them to take the test without consent or presence of counsel was in violation of our rights. They refused to allow either of us to call, Williams drew up an affidavit, saying he would submit without struggle if they would sign it. They refused. An assistant D.A. who was present said they were within their rights to demand the test: we pleaded as best we could to be allowed to call, to no avail. In the end they brought their chemical agents to each of our cells, gassed us until we passed out, shackled us with leg irons, restraining belt and chains, carried us to the M.T.A. and while we were retching, he took his test.

I am quite aware that my contentions as to legality depends on knowledge of all facts and interpretation, but there can be no doubt that what was done was immoral and a malicious assault upon our human dignity. Let's suppose they were right in demanding the blood. A sane, humane man would have consented to let at least one of us call, but the men of corrections are not men, they are gods beholden to no one and we the inmates are but caged apes without dignity or recourse when our rights are trampled. All we can do is return violence for violence, senseless brutality for the same, blindly striking out like caged beasts.

The point I am laboring to make is that if we, three men under indictment, allegedly under the protection of the courts, with brilliant dedicated attorneys at our disposal, and with the eyes of the public focused on all aspects of our case, can be brutalized, trampled upon in the manner I described, what chance does the everyday convict without benefit of any of the assets that we have, have of retaining his humanity and dignity in these pits?

The most pathetic thing was that the man who gave the order for the guards to gas us, said he was sorry but when asked why he would not sign the affidavit or allow us to call the attorneys, he said he did not have the authority, this from a 15 year veteran of corrections, former captain at San Quentin, program administrator of O-Wing, as cruel as all despots, as sorry as any man without any convictions other than power when he knows he must answer for his deeds. All of the events I described are true and can be corroborated.

Thank You For Your Time,
Jesse Phillips
O-Wing

FOLSOM STRIKE

In November of 1970, prisoners at Folsom (and some at Soledad) went on strike. Prison industries shut down; men remained in their cells. Prisoners wrote a manifesto of demands stating their grievances and suggested solutions. As the strike continued, many wrote letters describing its progress, the reaction of prison officials, the morale of the prisoners, and efforts made by the prison administration to end it.

This was the longest and best supported strike in California prison history; the men held out for nearly three weeks. None of the demands were granted.

THE FOLSOM PRISONERS MANIFESTO OF DEMANDS
AND
ANTI-OPPRESSION PLATFORM

WE THE IMPRISONED MEN OF FOLSOM PRISON SEEK AN END TO THE INJUSTICE SUFFERED BY ALL PRISONERS, REGARDLESS OF RACE, CREED, OR COLOR.

The preparation and content of this document has been constructed under the unified efforts of all races and social segments of this prison.

We the inmates of Folsom Prison totally and unlimitedly support the California state wide prison strike on November 3rd

1970, under the united effort for designated change in administrative prison practice and legislative policy.

It is a matter of documented record and human recognition that the administrators of the California prison system have restructured the institutions which were designed to socially correct men into THE FACIST CONCENTRATION CAMPS OF MODERN AMERICA.

DUE TO THE CONDITIONAL FACT THAT FOLSOM PRISON IS ONE OF THE MOST CLASSIC INSTITUTIONS OF AUTHORITATIVE INHUMANITY UPON MEN, THE FOLLOWING MANIFESTO OF DEMANDS ARE BEING SUBMITTED:

NOVEMBER 3, 1970

"MAN'S RIGHT TO KNOWLEDGE AND THE FREE USE THEREOF"

We the inmates of Folsom Prison have grown to recognize beyond the shadow of a doubt that because of our posture as prisoners and branded characters as alleged criminals, the administrators and prison employees no longer consider or respect us as human beings, but rather as domesticated animals selected to do their bidding in slave labor and furnished as a personal whipping dog for their sadistic, psycopathic hate.

We the inmates of Folsom Prison, say to you, the sincere people of society, the prison system of which your courts have rendered unto, is without question the authoritative fangs of a coward in power.

Respectfully submitted to the people as a protest to the vile and vicious slavemasters:
THE CALIFORNIA DEPARTMENT OF CORRECTIONS
THE CALIFORNIA ADULT AUTHORITY
THE CALIFORNIA STATE LEGISLATURE
THE CALIFORNIA STATE COURTS

THE UNITED STATES COURTS
AND THOSE WHO SUPPORT THIS SYSTEM OF INJUS-
TICE.

CALIFORNIA PRISONERS UNION

We the men of Folsom Prison have been committed to the State
Correctional Authorities by the people of society for the purpose
of correcting what has been deemed as social errors in behavior.
Errors which have classified us as socially unacceptable until
reprogrammed with new values and more thorough understanding as to our roles and responsibilities as members of the outside
community. The Folsom Prison program in its structure and
conditions have been engraved on the pages of this Manifesto of
Demands with the blood, sweat, and tears of the Inmates of this
prison.

The programs which we are submitted to under the facade of
rehabilitation, is relative to the ancient stupidity of pouring water
on a drowning man, inasmuch as we are treated for our hostilities
by our program administrators with their hostility as a medication.

In our efforts to comprehend on a feeling level an existence con-
trary to violence, we are confronted by our captors with violence.
In our efforts to comprehend society's code of ethics as to what
is fair and just, we are victimized by exploitation and the denial
of the celebrated due process of law.

In our peaceful efforts to assemble in dissent as provided under
this Nation's United States Constitution, we are in turn murdered,
brutalized and framed on various criminal charges because we
seek the rights and privileges of ALL AMERICAN PEOPLE.

In our efforts to intellectually expand in keeping with the outside world, through all categories of News Media, we are systematically restricted and punitively offended to isolation status when
we insist on our human rights to the wisdom of awareness.

We the inmates of this prison have vested the power of negotiation regarding settlement of the stipulated demands within the judgment and control of these four men of the outside world society:

SAL CANDELARIA,   (BROWN BERETS)
HUEY P. NEWTON,   (BLACK PANTHER PARTY)
CHARLES GARRY,   (3RD WORLD LEGAL DEFENSE COUNSEL)
REPRESENTATIVE   (FOR THE CALIFORNIA PRISONERS UNION TO BE DESIGNATED)

All and any negotiation will be conducted by Prison and State Authorities with these four men.

There shall be no convict committees.

AT 8:30 A.M. NOVEMBER 3RD, 1970, ALL CONVICT LABOR AND ASSIGNED ACTIVITY SHALL CEASE TO FUNCTION, WITH THE STIPULATED EXCEPTIONS OF:

(1) HOSPITAL WORKERS
(2) CULINARY WORKERS

ACTIVITY SHALL NOT RESUME UNTIL THE PRISON INMATE POPULATION HAVE RECEIVED DIRECTION FROM THE STIPULATED FOUR PERSON PANEL AS ABOVE MENTIONED, EITHER THROUGH RADIO, NEWS MEDIA, OR PERSONAL APPEARANCE.

MANIFESTO OF DEMANDS
11/3/70

1)

We demand the constitutional rights of legal representation at the time of all Adult Authority hearings, and the protection from the procedures of the Adult Authority whereby they permit no procedural safeguards such as an attorney for cross examination of witnesses, witnesses in behalf of the parolee, at parole revocation hearings.

2)

We demand a change in medical staff and medical policy and procedure. The Folsom Prison Hospital is totally inadequate, understaffed, prejudicial in the treatment of inmates. There are numerous "mistakes" made many times, improper and erroneous medication is given by untrained personnel. The emergency procedures for serious injury are totally absent in that they have no emergency room whatsoever; no recovery room following surgery which is performed by practitioners rather than board member surgeons. They are assisted by inmate help neither qualified, licensed, nor certified to function in operating rooms. Several instances have occurred where multiple injuries have happened to a number of inmates at the same time. A random decision made by the M.D. in charge as to which patient was the most serious and needed the one surgical room available. Results were fatal to one of the men waiting to be operated upon. This is virtually a death sentence to such a man who might have lived otherwise.

3)

We demand adequate visiting conditions and facilities for the inmates and families of Folsom prisoners. The visiting facilities at this prison are such as to preclude adequate visiting for the inmates and their families. As a result the inmates are permitted two hours, two times per month to visit with family and friends, which of course has to be divided between these people. We ask for additional officers to man the visiting room five days per week, so that everyone may have at least four hours visiting per month. The administration has refused to provide or consider this request in prior appeals using the grounds of denial that they cannot afford the cost of the extra officers needed for such change. However, they have been able to provide twelve new correctional officers to walk the gun rails of this prison, armed with rifles

and shotguns during the daytime hours when most of the prison
population is at work or attending other assignments. This is a
waste of the taxpayers money, and a totally unnecessary security
precaution.

4)

We demand that each man presently held in the Adjustment
Center be given a written notice with the Warden of Custody
signature on it explaining the exact reason for his placement in
the severely restrictive confines of the Adjustment Center.

5)

We demand an immediate end to indeterminate adjustment center
terms to be replaced by fixed terms with the length of time
served being terminated by good conduct and according to the
nature of the charges, for which men are presently being warehoused indefinitely without explanation.

6)

We demand an end to the segregation of prisoners from the mainline population because of their political beliefs. Some of the men
in the Adjustment Center are confined there solely for political
reasons and their segregation from other inmates is indefinite.

7)

We demand an end to political persecution, racial persecution,
and the denial of prisoners to subscribe to political papers, books
or any other educational and current media chronicals that are
forwarded through the United States Mail.

8)

We demand an end to the persecution and punishment of prisoners who practice the constitutional right of peaceful dissent. Prisoners at Folsom and San Quentin Prisons according to the California State Penal Code cannot be compelled to work as these

two prisons were built for the purpose of housing prisoners and there is no mention as to the prisoners being required to work on prison jobs in order to remain on the Mainline and/or be considered for release. Many prisoners believe their labor power is being exploited in order for the State to increase its economic power and continue to expand its correctional industries which are million dollar complexes, yet do not develop working skills acceptable for employment in the outside society, and which do not pay the prisoner more than the maximum sixteen cents per hour wage. Most prisoners never make more than six or eight cents per hour. Prisoners who refuse to work for the two to sixteen cent pay rate, or who strike, are punished and segregated without the access to the privileges shared by those who work; this is class legislation, class division, and creates class hostilities within the prison.

9)

We demand an end to the tear-gassing of prisoners who are locked in their cells. Such action led to the death of Willie Powell in Soledad Prison, in 1968 and of Fred Billinslea, on February 25th 1970 at San Quentin Prison. It is cruel and unnecessary.

10)

We demand the passing of a minimum and maximum term bill which calls for an end to indeterminate sentences whereby a man can be warehoused indefinitely, rehabilitated or not. That all prisoners have the right to be paroled after serving their minimum term instead of the cruel and unusual punishment of being confined beyond his minimum eligibility for parole, and never knowing the reason for the extension of time, nor when his time is completed. The maximum term bill eliminates indefinite life time imprisonment where it is unnecessary and cruel. Life sentences should not confine a man for longer than ten years, as seven years is the statute for a considered lifetime out of circulation and if a man cannot be rehabilitated after a maximum of ten years of constructive programs etc., then he belongs in a mental hygiene center, not a prison. Rescind Adult Authority Resolution 171, arbitrary fixing of prison terms.

11)

We demand that industries be allowed to enter the Institutions and employ inmates to work eight hours a day and fit into the category of workers for scale wages. The working conditions in prisons do not develop working incentives parallel to the money jobs in the outside society, and a paroled prisoner faces many contradictions on the job that adds to his difficulty to adjust. Those industries outside who desire to enter prisons should be allowed to enter for the purpose of employment placement.

12)

We demand that inmates be allowed to form or join Labor Unions.

13)

We demand that inmates be granted the right to support their own families; at present thousands of welfare recipients have to divide their checks to support their imprisoned relatives who without the outside support could not even buy toilet articles or food. Men working on scale wages could support themselves and families while in prison.

14)

We demand that correctional officers be prosecuted as a matter of law for shooting inmates, around inmates, or any act of cruel and unusual punishment where it is not a matter of life or death.

15)

We demand that all institutions who use inmate labor be made to conform with the state and federal minimum wage laws.

16)

We demand that all condemned prisoners, avowed revolutionaries and prisoners of war be granted political asylum in the countries

under the Free World Revolutionary Solidarity Pact, such as
Algeria, Russia, Cuba, Latin America, North Korea, North Vietnam, etc., and that prisoners confined for political reasons in
this country, until they can be exchanged for prisoners of war
held by America, be treated in accord with the 1954 Geneva
Convention; that they, their personal property be respected, and
allowed in their possession, and that they not be manacled.

17)

We demand an end to trials being held on the premises of San
Quentin Prison, or any other prison without the jury as stated
in the U.S. Constitution as being picked from the country of
the trial proceedings and of the peers of the accused; that being
in this case, other prisoners as the selected jurors.

18)

We demand an end to the escalating practice of physical brutality
being perpetrated upon the inmates of California State Prisons
at San Quentin, Folsom, and Soledad Prison in particular.

19)

We demand that such celebrated and prominent political prisoners as Reis Tijerina, Ahmad Evans, Bobby Seale, Chip Fitz-
gerald, Los Siete, David Harris, and the Soledad Brothers, be
given political asylum outside this country as the outrageous
slandering of the mass media has made it impossible either for a
fair trial or for a safe term to be served in case of conviction as
the forces of reactions and repressions will be forever submitting
them to threats of cruel and unusual punishment and death
wherever they are confined and throughout the length of their
confinement.

20)

We demand appointment of three lawyers from the California
Bar Association for full-time positions to provide legal assistance
for inmates seeking post-conviction relief, and to act as liaison

between the Administration and inmates for bringing inmate complaints to the attention of the Administration.

21)

We demand update of industry working conditions to standards as provided for under California law.

22)

We demand establishment of inmate workers insurance plan to provide compensation for work related accidents.

23)

We demand establishment of unionized vocational training program comparable to that of the Federal Prison System which provides for union instructors, union pay scale, and union membership upon completion of the vocational training course.

24)

We demand annual accounting of Inmate Welfare Fund and formulation of inmate committee to give inmates a voice as to how such funds are used.

25)

We demand that the Adult AUTHORITY Board appointed by the Governor be eradicated and replaced by a parole board elected by popular vote of the people. In a world where many crimes are punished by indeterminate sentences; where authority acts within secrecy and within vast discretion and gives heavy weight to accusations by prison employees against inmates, inmates feel trapped unless they are willing to abandon their desire to be independent men.

26)

We strongly demand that the State and Prison Authorities conform to recommendation #1 of the "Soledad Caucus Report," to wit,

"That the State Legislature create a fulltime salaried board of overseers for the State Prisons. The board would be responsible for evaluating allegations made by inmates, their families, friends, and lawyers against employees charged with acting inhumanely, illegally or unreasonably. The board should include people nominated by a psychological or psychiatric association, by the State Bar Association or by the Public Defenders Association, and by groups of concerned, involving laymen."

27)

We demand that prison authorities conform to the conditional requirements and needs as described in the recent released Manifesto from the Folsom Adjustment Center.

28)

We demand an immediate end to the agitation of races relations by the prison administrations of this state.

29)

We demand that the California Prison System furnish Folsom Prison with the services of Ethnic Counselors for the needed special services of Brown and Black population of this prison.

30)

We demand an end to the discrimination in the judgement and quota of parole for Black and Brown People.

31)

We demand that all prisoners be present at the time that their cells and property are being searched by the correctional officers of state prisons.

MESSAGE FROM A BROTHER IN FOLSOM
(Wednesday, November 4)

The situation at this time is that we have approximately 2100 people who did not work or function in any programmatic capacity today. We had approximately 152 people who did fulfill their work and vocational assignments. However, it is our feeling that within the next 24 hours we will have 100% response.

We have had three or four incidents where individuals have been committed to isolation for discussing the strike and for circulating literature in this area. As it is escalated and the anxieties rise a little higher, we do expect more suppression from the administration. We have been peaceable and orderly; we don't desire destructive things, we don't want a violent thing. We really want to raise the issue on a peaceful level. We feel that this way it should maintain the respect of the administration, as well as the people.

November 8, 1970

Thomas K. Clark
Box No. B-14975
Represa, California 95671

Patti Roberts

Comrade Mine:

We have been virtually starved for the past four days, and if things aren't back to "normal" by tomorrow I suspect it will become worse.

It's difficult at this point to say with any degree of certainty whether or not the strike will fold, but I can definitely state, emphatically announce, that there is more tenacity and a greater sense of purpose in the atmosphere at this moment than I ever believed possible in this particular institution.

The pre-historic are not often revolutionary. (smile)

You wouldn't believe the sandwiches they are feeding us . . . I'm looking at them and don't believe it. They offered our building (which by the way is the most militant strike-wise) a shower tonight. Less than a third took advantage of it. A good sign.

Everything will hang or fall on what this building does in the morning. If they hang tough tomorrow . . . baby, we got um . . . and I ain't jiving.

They have "five" rifle packing pigs on the gun rail . . . is that too much? I guess that is designed to intimidate us.

Let us hope that tomorrow finds Convict Power still in action.

They cut all outside communication as we suspected, but didn't pick up the private radios . . . Yeah, plenty stupid!

Take care . . .

All Power to the People

Folsom Prison
November 9, 1970

Dear Fay and Patti:

We're holding it—pretty good, considering the intimidation. We heard on the radio today—a statement from Warden craven Cravens that 50% of the men came out to work today—but let me tell you, he got his "figures" a mite confused. The men here —there was no confusion or terrorization like he claimed—complete calm. And the 50% he spoke of, all wanting to get back to his work—6%. Off this tier of 50 men 3 went to breakfast. And all that after being locked up 24 hours a day and eating only two cold sack lunches of two balony sandwiches at 10:00 and 3:00.

As we sat here for the rest of today (without eating—since we wouldn't go to the mess hall, he wouldn't even give us sack lunches), Bob and I listened for complaints, but never heard one. We have plenty to do—our writing and books to keep us from getting hungry—but most of these guys, what have they got? Nothing. Let me tell you, my faith and love and admiration for my brother convicts went up about 500%, God bless them, they took it like men—making Bob marvel. "I wonder how many street people could take this sort of 24-hour intimidation without squawking?"

Today, would you believe—our sack lunch came and inside— a candy bar: Hollywood. Those things they pulled off the market because of rodent hair and filth. Most of us threw the dirty things over the gunrail; one guy's smashed a window. To hell with food if it comes to *that*. We know he's slick, but he can go only so far, and we feel it—the people is after his ass—and so are you. God bless you, and God bless the future. Power to YOU and the People.

Yours,
James Williamson

Folsom
November 17, 1970

Hello Out There Fay and Patterson,

When I first reached this street in Folsom, I deeply adjusted to it, and at the same time did not adjust to it at all. I adjusted to Folsom Prison as one adjusts to the probability that a man in a casket is dead, and I never adjusted to it as one would never adjust to the theory that one is one's self dead simply because one happens to find one's self in a casket.

"Water! Hot Water!"

We heard the call down the tier, and there goes W., starting his early morning water brigade. It's been that way since the strike (still called a lock-in by Craven), his getting up early to take care of his brothers. Hot water. There isn't much of it around here. By some stroke of genius W. got hold of the plumber two days before the purported strike and for a few packs of smokes had hot water piped into this cell, 1616. Now we are the most popular men on the fourth tier—thank goodness; strings run from here to several cells (each direction), all pulling little plastic containers of hot water for coffee, for tea, maybe to shave with or wash the feet, who knows? On one side, 1615, an Indian, Pawnee from Muscogee, Oklahoma; on the other side a Chicano, from somewhere—1617. Next to him (1618), The Senator, and his Watuisi friend—good black men, all have to be served. "If we only had us a yellow man up here we'd be serving the whole world," W. laughs in his sardonic wit, and hollers, "Water! Water!"

Well, it won't always be like this—but even stupidity and prisons and jailors must be observed, and sometimes even a little admired for their callous indifference to humanity. Have some fun for us.

Yours,
Jim Williamson

Folsom
November 20, 1970

Sisters:

Here is a report on what's happening. Pig Walter E. Craven said in regards to the strike that revolutionaries who are representing the people here at Folsom State Prison were using the people here at Folsom State Prison for political reasons, and to antagonize the public. He went on to said we should think as an individual and go to work etc.

Comrades, Walter E. Craven is a technique at manipulating. That remark was a insult to all revolutionaries. Then this pig Walter E. Craven said if the mans don't go to work he will have to make a big isolation out of Folsom State Prison. Comrades, this pig think he God. He call that a psychological threat.

Comrades, what the pig is saying is this—no exercise, no privileges, some kind of restricted diet, and up to the hell confinement. But we say to the pig Suck!! Long and deep.

Howard

Folsom
Nov. 25, 1970

Dear Mrs. Stender:

. . . The pigs have begun "nightriding" as a tactic of intimidation and harassment of strikers. Last night around three o'clock in the morning they brought two prisoners into the segregation section totally nude with an escort of five pigs wielding clubs and heavy flashlights . . .

Viva La Huelga!
Pancho

Folsom
9-23-70

Mrs. Stender,

. . . believe me not only is this place not fit for people but (excuse the expression) this place is not fit for a dog. Down on the first floor in this adjustment center the isolation cells are not fit for anyone to stay in. There is no light in the cell, the cell is dark all the time. There is a officer come by and tries to start confusion between the races by saying "now aren't you a fool for going along with the nigger strike!" . . .

Gilbert

Folsom
November 24, 1970

Faithful Comrade:

The strike was broken *not* because the prisoners had become disenchanted. The Collective Spirit and optimism were too real to make me believe that the prisoners went to work as a result of disillusionment. Two-thousand men don't strike for 19 days and then suddenly become disenchanted. Only the most naive of fools would believe that such a thing could happen. Therefore, it is only logical that devious means were employed to break the strike.

It is clear as crystal that Craven used political deception and brute force to get the prisoners to go back to work. On the 23rd of November (Monday morning the day the strike was broken) the prison pigs, armed with rifles and wooden clubs, stopped in front of each man's cell and ordered each man back to work. Of course the order was weighted down with the threat of violence. Not wanting to be shot or clubbed to death, the prisoner naturally complied with the pigs' vicious method of brute force.

In building one, one of Craven's inmate agents drew up several reactionary leaflets and circulated them throughout the building (Building one is where "Kitchen Row" is located). The leaflets, which were passed from cell to cell by the inmates, said that the Kitchen Workers were supposed to go back to work so that the prisoners could start eating hot meals. Because so many legitimate leaflets and notes were being circulated throughout Building One, the inmates in that building naturally assumed that those reactionary leaflets were the real thing. This was the method used to get the Kitchen Workers to go back to work.

The day before the strike was broken, Craven, in an announcement over the prison radio, said that you and your colleagues were connected with communist organizations and that the strike was part of a communist conspiracy. However, I don't think that these slanderous remarks had too much of an adverse effect on the prisoners. Perhaps a few prisoners used Craven's lies as an excuse to go back to work. (Paper is scarce and I'm running out of room.) I hope this information will be of some use to you.

ALL POWER TO THE PEOPLE,
Hassan

Folsom
November 21, 1970

Dear Fay and Patti:

This letter ought to be called, "Breaking Up the Cement So the Flowers can Grow!"

There is the "Soledad Three," now we have the "Folsom Four": Jim Williamson, Manual Chavez, Garry Roblas, and Cezar Moore: four Folsom prisoners who did no wrong; men who sometimes earlier (before the Folsom strike) were asked to (and agreed to) meet the National Lawyer's Guild, *or* the press (or anybody) on a discussion of California Penology. Not on a collective basis—personally—to discuss world conditions.

But somebody had to break up the cement so the flowers would grow. It was only later, early Friday Morning, Nov. 20, 1970, when Lt. W., Guard W., C., and two more goons (squadders) burst into their cells at 3:00 a.m., stood them on the tier for an hour in their underwear, then billyclubs in hand marched them to R & R, dressed them in white denims and tossed them handcuffed feet and hands into the back of the Folsom laundry van, that they knew it—that flowers do not by themselves through cement grow.

It is a good thing we have no Society for the Prevention of Cruelty to Convicts, or Lt. W. & his boys would be out of business today. I mean the slay ride from Folsom to CMC East San Louis Obispo was great; prisoners ought to be punished that way—teach them humility and etc—but by God, did the trip have to last that long—or did W. & his Goons (all four of them) take the long way around? So they wouldn't have to hurry back to Folsom and work in the tag plant?

We never know about those things, but it is all right—nobody got hurt, and a man ought to experience certain things, keeps him on his toes. A little hungry maybe, cold yes, but not pain that won't go away in a few days, no memory that won't last over a life time—at least for a writer, a man who *needs* to experience things.

Madness—gladness, why does the human spirit demand it?

None of the Folsom Four started the strike, none could have ended it, but before the van ride was over, all the men were less prejudiced toward those who did start the strike. Or did the strike start itself? Was that van ride part of the Dept's. conscience on review? Somewhere in the manifesto there was a provision against arbitrary treatment whose meaning began to take on more meaning as the trip progressed.

A man is what he remembers; he is also what he forgets. I want to try to remember some of that van ride, but before I do, this can be said about all human beings: such treatment of people (said to be human), as sides of beef, is a sort of intimidation that always back fires on the perpetrators in the end, and before that van ride was completed, 14 hours later, all the prisoners said to a man: "If this trip is necessary to prove cruelty exists in the Department of Corrections, then I would have volunteered for it." One man said, "I would have run along behind the van, or they could have dragged me down here if it helps bust up Folsom and makes the flowers grow." Somebody invented a beautiful song on the spot, "Brigade of the Brown Paper Bags" and it was sung immediately with fervor and spirit.

Viva la flowers—let the concrete go!

For Mr. Procunier (who gave orders for the van ride) I want to remember it well; first the cold; lying bound handcuffed, on the ribbed floor of the van, how it bit into the bones! It wasn't long till the feet couldn't feel the cold—the tight bite of the leg cuffs took care of that. But the back could, the arms and legs. I want to remember the turning and twisting of halfnude bodies looking for a soft spot on the metal floor; of the blue lips that made no *outward* complaint; the torture of gasoline fumes, motion sickness from riding upside down backwards; the musings of the two van guards, separated by steel mesh: "Don't catch anything on fire back there, we'll jump out and let her burn."

I want to remember the prisoners were more in danger of freezing to death than burning up; the hours, the miles, hundred after hundred; how the van accompanied from the rear by another car with Lieutenant W. and another guard, stopped off for a hot breakfast *somewhere* on the road, and came back to the hungry, cold prisoners, patting their bellies and asking them, "Why, how do you guys feel?"

Well, how do four men feel lying trapped and chained in their own spitum, kidneys breaking, backbone trembling? Not a peep from the prisoners; their teeth always chatter like that. Or maybe they were too warm to speak, or too tired. Or too disgusted with raw humanity!

Madness! Insanity! Each of those prisoners will have to live next door to someone someday—but how would you like for one to marry your sister?

A writer must forget, but it is better if he remembers it, and even a good case of sadism must be admired, it *deserves* to be, because only through tolerance—love and hate, good and evil— does man grow in perspective; out of the evil of the human race has come some of its greatness: Joan of Arc, Jesus Christ, John Brown, Gandhi are a few examples that come to mind. No doubt about it, out of prisons such as Folsom will emergy another saint some day, somebody who will be able to break up the cement so the flowers can grow. But in the meantime, four men took a van ride—what that busted up, I'll never know—and they took it singing and shouting and cold—because in their hearts they know it still—somebody *has* to ride the vans if the cement is ever to go.

Yours always,
James Williamson

P.S. . . . If you get the chance, see somebody on the Budget Analysis Committee (Ways and Means) and find out why the Department of Corrections has such a surplus of men that they can use four of them for a two day trip with four prisoners. I mean this would be interesting in light of the Department always wanting a budget increase in view of Governor Reagan's cuts every year. It cost the people $400 to transfer four men from Folsom to San Luis Obispo—where is the other money being spent?

GETTING TOGETHER

Folsom
Feb. 6, 1971

Dear Comrade:

As I related to you today, it is precarious approaching [white groups], but as I said *we* are willing, if for no other reason than to free our forces from a senseless struggle against those who are not our true foe. Vendettas grow easily and die hard. There are many memories of fallen comrades on both sides. But the strife and the bitterness has only benefited the enemies of both camps. The forces of reactionarianism are the only victors. Two hundred years of foolishness is no justification for continuing to be fools, I feel now that a mere coalition of convenience is not enough and I shall attempt to do as much as I can to coalesce the alliance into a viable force for common efforts against the common foe for the good of all. I feel now that it is possible to develop a *class* loyalty even if not a *revolutionary* consciousness. Prisoners are a specific and degraded class. Class loyalty and consciousness is definitely achievable. Some of the comrades agree with this last analysis and other do not but all are devoted to advancing the movement "by any means necessary." We therefore are going to move in the direction I have outlined with revolutionary resolve.

All power to the people,
Comrade Robert Charles Jordan

Folsom
Sept. 14, 1970

Dear Sister:

Our primary interest is to establish a Chicano Organization at Folsom that will work seeking solutions to Chicano problems, and implementing programs for the self-improvement of the Chicano convict.

I will briefly state the steps we have taken up to the present time. All this has taken almost two (2) years—a reason why more and more voices are being raised everyday for a direct confrontation either by a demonstration or a strike by the Chicanos.

We prepared a Constitution and By-Laws to govern the group. This was submitted to the Warden. After a length of time he denied permission to form said organization. Thereafter two meetings were held with Mr. Faustman, Associate Warden, relative to the denial. He suggested that we change our constitution in certain respects to comply and conform with a Department of Corrections policy directive regarding self-improvement groups. This was done. It was then submitted to the Warden for reconsideration: Again it was denied.

Our next step was to ask permission from Mr. R. K. Procunier, Director of the Department of Corrections. We mailed Mr. Procunier a letter requesting that he grant us permission to form the organization and enclosed a copy of the constitution together with a petition signed by about three hundred Chicanos. An associate answered telling us that Mr. Procunier was on vacation but would consider it on his return. Well, finally we received an answer from Mr. Procunier stating that he left such decisions to the Warden, and if he denied permission then it was final.

After due consideration we hit on another tactic on how to bring the issue up again before the Warden. We approached it through the Prison Education Department—that is, we went to the Student Advisory Council (inmates) asking their support for a Chicano Cultural Group under the auspices of the Education Department (this was no longer the same type of organiza-

tion we first envisioned). In any case, after getting the run around
—not by the inmates but by staff responsible for the Education
Department—we finally were able to draw up our proposals to
present to the Student Advisory Council. Again after waiting
sometime we obtained their support and the proposals were submitted to the Warden. Needless to say that after he kept said
proposals for a while he denied them.

The above is but an idea of what we have encountered in terms
of administrative opposition. Other things were done but these
are the most important. Whether our methods could have been
better is now immaterial, the point is that we have complied with
all their rules and have gotten absolutely nowhere.

Manuel Joe Chavez

Folsom
Sept. 14, 1970

Dear Sister Stender:

Let me bring you up to date, sister. During the Chicano Mora-
torium in Los Angeles—which turned into a police riot (they
call it a "Mexican-American" riot)—two Chicano brothers were
killed by the police. The Chicanos here wanted to honor our
brothers, one was Ruben Salazar, so we asked permission from
the catholic priest at Folsom for a service in memory of our
brother and that he let a Chicano eulogize our brothers before
the service. We were even denied this! In any event, our black
brothers, the Black Muslims, offered to let us honor our brother
at their service. We gladly accepted this opportunity. Two Chicanos spoke at said service to a chapel (Mosque) filled with
both Blacks and Chicanos. You can imagine what the administration thought about this. That Blacks and Chicanos got together has perplexed the administration, and they apparently take
this as constituting a threat to the *status quo* and to their way
of operating.

Next we wrote a letter to the Warden, signed by two hundred

and fifty Chicanos, asking for an interview with a committee of ten to discuss Chicano problems, and to see if we could obtain permission to celebrate the 16th of September (Mexican Independence Day). The Warden has not given us the requested interview, but he did talk to one of the members of the committee. In fact, he told the Chicano that because we got together with our black brothers we were trying to start an insurrection at the institution and that he didn't like it.

This brings us to a matter that might have repercussions: The Black Muslims have invited us to attend their service on Saturday, September 19th, as a means of celebrating Mexican Independence Day. There will be *Two* Chicano speakers, Henry Castro and Jess Cancino. Since the Warden has already expressed his displeasure with us having a service together with the Black Muslims, it is possible that the speakers will be locked up or possibly some of the Chicanos that they have down as being instrumental in trying to form a Chicano organization, including myself.

Que viva La Raza!
Manuel Joe Chavez

Folsom
Sept., 1970

Comrade Mine:

I cannot put into words my joy at the prospect of brotherhood between our two families of color. To think that we might finally put an end to the senseless waste of life and talent, and at the same time put a stop to the vicious exploitation of the Department of Correction, directed at our family of color, is an emotional joy which transcends my ability to employ words. I can only say that it is a day which shall forever remain among my most precious memories of positive action.

Peace . . . . and take care.
Thomas

Folsom
Sept. 13, 1970

Dearest Comrade:

There was a eulogy held here at Folsom prison for Ruben Salazar by a large percentage of the brown and black population. Due to the fact that racial solidarity and harmony is *not acceptable by the prison administration* the following incidents occurred:

On date of Sept. 10th. One of the Chicano brothers who attended the brown and black eulogy was confronted while in his cell at building #3, which is on the main-line of prison population, by three correctional pigs. The brother was Padilla #A-60132. He was dragged from his cell by these three pigs, and physically beaten while standing on the tier, was then kicked repeatedly down three flights of stairs, then taken to the hospital to be medically cleared for isolation purpose. And what appeared to be a very serious condition was placed in a stripped cell incommunicado. At this time we have no knowledge as to whether he is dead or alive.

On the date of Sept. 10th. One of the Chicano speakers at the eulogy, brother Jose Annatt (A-52561), was attacked by three correctional pigs, chained and shackled and *physically thrown* on a C.D.C. bus for a destination listed as (Susan-Ville) but true destination *unknown*.

On the date of Sept. 11th. Warden Craven of this prison confronted Jose Castro and stated that he would tolerate no form of unity between black and brown prisoners, and would crush it according to our famous phrase "by any means necessary."

Due to the fact that the prison Chaplin refused to let the Chicano population hold a eulogy for Ruben Salazar, the inmate Muslim Minister here at Folsom, gave the time and so-called privilege allowed for muslim services to the community efforts for this eulogy. As the result of the Muslim Minister's cooperation in this "humane matter" the warden Craven also confronted the Folsom Nation of Islam, and stated that any and all Chicano participation in any Muslim services of the future were definitely forbidden by he and the total prison administration.

ALL POWER TO THE PEOPLE.

<u>YOURS IN STRUGGLE, YOURS IN PEACE.</u>

Bro. Alfred Hassan

Soledad
October 16, 1970

Dear Mrs. Stender:

It is my reflection that certain people are making an honest effort to create better conditions within the total prison establishment in the State of California. This effort has been centered around the injustices perpetrated against Blacks within the prison system. Yet this is only one side of the coin. What of the injustices committed against ignorant Whites of the poor class of people who enter prison, only to be inculcated with the various propaganda of Racism and Nazism, by prison guards who maintain, sustain by feeding literature and support (even weapons) to the same.

Until here recently, I was buried in the nebulous shadows of such virulent diatribe. My first lesson came from a prison guard who started me on the way saying "Boy, you ain't a man until you done stuck a nigger," a fictional example but too close to the truth, and how hard we all struggle to be men, or what we feel that man should be like. For a time I lived suspended in the full current of "prison Nazism," but at the expense of a constant thought lurking within my human confine that I had been pushed beyond the antics of self-control, and was being swept away violently by the hand of prison officials against people: warm, thinking, talking human beings as myself, and all this really against my immediate will.

One day I decided to regain possession of my own mind and become responsible for my own thoughts and actions. I left the Nazi "trip" and acquired new friends, some of which are black. For this change, this rebellion against the racist demagogues of the prisons, I was hounded by them, guards (certain) demanded

I remove the Nazi swastikas tattooed on my body or my death would be arranged. I left it on in defiance of them all. When it became obvious that my stand to be self-assertive was complete and void of fear, with a irrelevant attitude towards their intimidation set against me, prison officials removed me from the main line and rehoused me in "O" wing, with a "program," in fear that my stand would influence other misled poor Whites to throw off the shackles of racist orientation and seek unity and friendship with Blacks.

Yes, Mrs. Stender, my own situation may hopefully improve. But only were I to turn back to that fog where I, like other poor Whites, become tools to be wielded in the hands of prison officials. I can't turn back, I won't turn back. I see my job (thanks to daily conversations with Brother Earl Satcher) as exerting every ounce of strength in me to elevate the political consciousness of my poor White brothers in an effort to save them from the pitfalls of prison entrapment and show them that where one man is denied freedom so are all men; that justice must fall like an acorn from a tree, in one straight line, and that the struggle of Blacks and Chicanos is the struggle to free all people from the yoke of imperialist modern slavery.

William B. Thomason

Soledad
Oct. 20, 1970

Dear Sister,

I received your letter today dated the 19th and it would be difficult for anyone person to imagine how much I appreciate its arrival. Believe me, at this very moment I'm trying to not blink my eye lids for contemplating the tears that might stream down the cheeks of my face: as I read your letter and ask myself why has it taken so long to discover the people? Maybe the way I feel as I write this letter may only be compared with the way the "Red Man" felt when he streamed into the North American Continent on a vast migration down through the Alaskan Con-

tinent and suddenly run smack into a whole new world of beauty;
a world where even the call of a lonely meadow-lark rendered
a sacred thing of beauty and fascination! It may seem hard to
believe, but I just stood at the bars of my cell and shouted "All
power to the People!" Brother James Wagner (of the "7") called
back "right on! Whats the matter down there?" and Brother Earl
Satcher answered better than I could ever hope to. He said "I'm
drunk from the eating of the Locust and wild honey from the
suspended garden of the third world!" Well, possibly I am, yet
again it may be that I am happy and thankful that humanity is
alive and doing well.

Related to this, as Brother Earl (whom I owe my present state
of political and social awareness to) has stated in the nightly
political orientation sessions that he draws us into here on isolation. (One of the main reasons I shall refuse to move upstairs.)
As Brother Earl stated, "The battle here in America, free world
and prisons, has never been predicated upon the premise of Black
& White per se with respect to the people, but actually a battle
between *ideologies.*" In this statement I agree. Because people
are killed by power structures in efforts to stagnate or control
challenging ideologies is opposition to them. The Jan. 13th happening [the shooting of three black prisoners in an exercise yard
at Soledad on January 13, 1970, by a guard] strongly suggests
an intensification of a systematic method of elimination perpetrated against the revolutionary and anti-racist ideology spreading throughout the Black psyche of the Black prisoner that is
now beginning to take hold of the white and Chicanos in State
prisons. Therefore, I readily can see the Black Struggle as the
vanguard conducive to the freedom of all oppressed. Besides I
rather think they, the Blacks, have priority as predicated upon
many many years of oppression that Whites as myself have not
ever known . . .

> All power to the People
> A true Brother
> William B. Thomason

Soledad
Oct. 20, 1970

Fay Stender,

I was called today on behalf of the people, and was found wanting. In my humble way, I shall try to explain, for as you noted, my thinking has slowly been changing due to conversations with Brother Earl S., although I feel I'm not qualified to call him Brother anymore. As I recently explained I had to do "20" days in isolation in "O" wing. It was discussed between Earl S. and myself, and I decided that I would refuse to go upstairs to do my program, and try to stay downstairs . . . and also to keep from having to go under the gun.

This evening at app. 5:30 p.m. two officers approached my cell and told me I was going upstairs, either the hard or easy way. I once again refused. Mr. Earl had advised me not to physically fight back, so I didn't. When the sergeant entered my cell he placed a tear gas cannister app. 6 inches from my face and told me to extend my hands to be handcuffed. I placed the Bible I was reading upon my bunk, and did as instructed . . . Could you please try and convey my feelings to Mr. Earl and try and explain the situation to him, as we cannot communicate. Thank you for this, and I shall always be in your debt.

Yours truly,
William B. Thomason

Soledad
Oct. 24, 1970

Dear Fay:

I've received your letter this Oct. 22, 1970, letting me know the present situation and what to expect of the future.

I am with understanding related to the conditions concerning the White Brother W. B. Thomason. As concerning this brother: Several days ago, the prison guards came on isolation and forced the Brother to move to the program section of O-Wing, under the threat of being maced. The "forced" move was predicated on the fact that the brother Billy had decided, after many nights of attending the political dialogue sessions we hold here on isolation, to remain on isolation as a means of protesting the insipid, and racist conditions and injustices perpetrated against prisoners, especially Black, here at Soledad Prison: And further as a means to dramatize and protest his innocence of any wrong doing for which he was confined in the isolation cell blocks for punishment. Prison officials were shocked that the brother has become a "free thinking human being" after the ignorance and confusion caused by the Neo-Amerikan Nazism inculcated in his mind by the prison officials. And from which many many white prisoners yet suffer from. It is in that context we must see that W. B. Thomason has become the first "White" at this prison to be persecuted, as he is presently being, solely because of his new awakening unto a revolutionary-Political frame of mind. Per adventure you are aware of this fact via communications from them. Although he isn't as articulate as other brothers, his heart and mind is striving in the correct direction. Of course, when he was present on isolation I tried to aid him with what little help I was able. I know you understand. Because I deeply feel the beauty of the third world should be open to all who sincerely seek its reality and with to labor at its building.

> Sincerely
> A brother in arms and truth
> Earl

> Soledad
> Oct. 27, 1970

Dear Sister:

I feel compelled to try and explain my last communications with you.

Since that letter, I communicated with the afore mentioned party, (Satcher) and was greatly relieved, if not elated, to find I had not suffered a loss of stature in his eyes. I have come to compare myself with one who has lived his life in a state of un-aware slumber and am just awakening to the real world and to the injustices, being perpetrated by man against his fellow man.

In closing, I wish to express my humble thanks for your time, and understanding, and sincerely hope I will be able to meet you in the near future.

Your Faithful Brother
William B. Thomason

Folsom
Dec. 30, 1970

Dear Comrade:

Sister it is almost unbelievable to contemplate the rapport be-tween the different ethnic or racial groups that exists here in this Adjustment Center. The change in thought processes that neces-sarily preceded this rapport are equally unbelieveable when viewed in the context of the racial and clique animosities that were existent just a year ago when I first arrived here. The animosity has dissipated to no more than a murmur in the background. That is not to say that there is total racial or clique acceptance, but the people here have awakened to the fact that the pigs have been using race as a *weapon* in a carefully calculated and systematic scheme to continue to oppress and suppress *all* in these tombs. Political awareness pervades the very air here. Political dialectics are the common topics of conversation, replacing pimping, rob-bing, and hustling as the main interest. Frantz Fanon, Mao Tse-Tung, Regis Debray, Che and Marx have replaced Louis La'mour, Max Brand. Due to a habeas action I filed in the Su-perior Court a couple of months ago we now get the Berkeley Tribe, the Barb, and any other underground press issues. The Tribe has supplanted the Sacramento Bee, etc., as sources of information and topical reference. There are those of us here who just a year ago had truly what could only be called criminal minds and outlooks, and to whom acts of rape, murder, homo-sexual assaults, robbery, and general violence—against the people

—were less than nothing and were common conduct. *All* of *that* has even changed. There are these, who just last year had the above criminal mentality and disposition and callous disregard for the lives and/or persons of the people, who would today lay down their lives for the people and for the good of the movement. The harmony here is real and is of an enduring nature. There will undoubtedly be instances of racial incidents between individuals: human beings are human beings and will act according to impulse, etc., and no accord will ever be totally unmarred. But the unity is real and it grows stronger everyday.

All Power to the People
Comrade Robert

ANOTHER POINT OF VIEW

Dear Faye,

After reading the series of articles on the Calif. prisons in the Sac. Bee, and also an article by one Eve Pell, concerning racial persecution of the Blacks by the pigs and white racist pig collaboratees at Soledad Prison I wanted to puke. I have never in all the time I have spent in A.C.'s participated in the petty name calling that goes on among the different races but I have heard it and it is never one sided and often as not is kicked off by Blacks. I attempted to explain this to you when we spoke a few months ago but obviously you are not really concerned with reality. I had hoped that with your help we could start bringing people together and put an end to his madness but it seems I have been very naieve. You people can't even get together outside. The so called movement is a big joke. The Blacks, whites, and Browns spend so much time bickering amongst there respective groups and organizations they haven't got time to concentrate on the pigs who are killing them left and right. The only people who are together are the oppressors.

Look if you people want to take the position that the racial conflict in the prisons is all the fault of white racist savages and those who identify with same. (That was real smooth) that's OK with me because I personally have never been affected by any of it. But I don't like to be used and lied to. I have been singing your praises and telling all the savages that unity is whats happening and you people turn right around and print all that one sided bull shit and we are right back to the same spot we started from. I can't quite make up my mind wether you are unbelievably stupied, or just plain rotten and decittful, but in either case I have nothing but contempt for you. Personally I don't want to hear anymore of your shit, and you can be assured that everyone I know in the system is going to hear how you use people. I'm sure you all had a good chuckle when you received the letters and other documents from the various people you gamed on, they were very clumsy and crude but they expressed themselves the best way they knew how and they were sincere. When you put your trust in someone as a friend you are defenseless. Tell comrade I wish him the very best but don't send no more bastards like you to me again.

Robert Francis Butler

"When the prison gates open the real dragons will fly out."

Ho Chi Minh

While prison is unfit for human shelter and a cruel mockery of the human condition, it nonetheless provides an ideal atmosphere for revolutionary education. Nowhere in society are the contradictions of the Government's system of justice so glaring as they are in prison. In prison, oppression and brutality are not camouflaged by the subtle trappings of political dissent and social concessions. Even in the wretched Black Colonies of America, where oppression runs rampant, at least the oppressor makes an attempt to cover up his bloody trail. But in prison, the barbaric persecution by the oppressor is raw and naked . . .

Alfred Hassan

Soledad
July 23, 1969

Dear Fay,

By experience Fay, I should not be surprised at the attitude of those who are not, in fact, our comrades in the battle for human liberation; even the liberal bourgeoisie (fellow-travellers) live in a world which is far removed from the agony of the oppressed; especially that of this repressed existence—for all their pretense to "understanding" and "humanitarianism." Yet, even *knowing* this I continue to extend my hand, asking not so much for "assistance" but for something far more universal—something *far* removed from the caricature that is the product resulting from the outsider's interpretation. Time after time the intensity of my expression (and I admit that I am very *intense* . . . not only about my life, but that of my brothers and sisters . . . about the need *not* to compromise our revolution, nor compromise our relationships to one another) is distorted and damned— Why do I go on? . . .

Because you're a dreamer, an incredible dreamer, with a tiny spark hidden somewhere inside you which cannot die, which even you cannot kill or quench and which tortures you horribly because all the odds are against its continued burning. In the midst of the foulest decay and putrid savagery, this spark speaks to you of beauty, of human worth and kindness, of goodness, of greatness, of heroism, of martyrdom, and it speaks to you of love.

(Soul on Ice.)

It is this spark Fay which creates the inferno; the raging, searching force which constantly (almost compulsively) drives you on in the face of the most bitter betrayals of your trust and "ideals"—that which gives you the balls to strive to create from this dream a reality of humanity—of love between all of us as brothers and sisters. Something which is both an intense love and a deep fraternal comradeship.

It you are like us (the product of America's social abortion) you start from only an unbelievable conception of yourself as having some intrinsic worth—though reality, it seems, works day and night to interpret this as madness; at least as a paranoiac delusion! Finally, you suffer through the years (for Eldridge 9— for myself 7) until you find that in spite of the system which has tried to destroy you that you are a *human being* who CAN care honestly about other people; who CAN love honestly and beyond the point of "lust"; that life is bigger than you are, yet, that without your concern and your desire to make it better for everyone, it is threatened with destruction—moral and physical. Your New Found Worth then becomes intrinsically tied to the worth of others, not only those like yourself who have suffered so long this nauseating repression of the mind, but to those who in spite of their perpetuation of the oppression, are also Victims.

You now have *something to live for* where you previously had nothing: Do you have any idea of what that means to those like us? To now know from day-to-day that life has a meaning other than alienation and oppression? That suddenly all the suffering is bearable—even rationally acceptable so long as we have a reason to go on; go on in the belief that *we have the power to do something about it!* It is beyond the description of "Being Re-born!" . . .

I close-off for now, thanking you for your kindness.

Sincerely,
Michael B. McCarthy

From the Revolutionary Prisoner
For: Patti
By Alfred Hassan

Dear Comrade:

The decision to struggle for liberation is a compulsory one. The historic process of subjecting a people to misery and anguish under oppression can only be broken by revolution; and that means, if the people without freedom are ever to gain it from those who keep freedom from them by force and terror, then they are going to have to seize it with their own hands.

The world is dividing into two opposing camps: the oppressed and the oppressors. Some people can choose the camp they'll belong to; their struggle is ideological. But I, being born a Black Man, was born in the camp of the oppressed with a history of 400 years of struggle that had affected me before my birth, a struggle born and waged as a "historically determined necessity."

Trying to grow up in a capitalist society that uses racism as its chief weapon, I came into conflict with every institution set up to control my life and the destiny of my people. A capitalist society is so full of contradictions that everyone in it is in conflict with someone else. But different conflicts lead people to different places, and my conflicts were numerous enough to lead me to prison.

Prison is when my education began earnest, where I learned more about the source of my (our) conflicts; and it is where I began to look at my history and the history of other oppressed people in the world and how they set out to resolve their conflicts through the process of resistant struggle and revolutionary wars of varying types, depending on time, circumstance, condition, place and history. From the beginning of my incarceration, I found others in "captive detention" who sought the same answers as myself, and we looked for them together. We grew as the movement on the streets here in Babylon grew. We were always under constant observation by those responsible for keeping us, "the enemy." But this observation did not disturb us because we would use this as our "academy" and study because theory precedes practice—and "preparation is key." When we were released we'd take what solutions we had with us to the community. But as the movement outside drew world attention, it also drew the attention of the wardens, and they began to associate the fact that Malcolm X was a convict and that we were convicts, that Malcolm X studied and that we were studying. Then the *natural* was identified solely with Rap and became the "Rap Brown haircut," or the "football helmet" as the pigs at Soledad prison call it. Everytime a natural-headed nigger popped up on this T.V. screen or on the front page of a paper, he had a gun in his hand. So the pigs associated this with us again and we became more of a threat to them now than ever before. We were no longer just "niggers" but "niggers with guns." And the *natural* was outlawed in every pen; they threatened us with "the hole," with force, with forcible haircuts and everything to keep us from walking around the joint with our *naturals* booming because they kept seeing in their minds "them niggers with guns coming after them."

The time passed when Black Men could use the prison facilities as just a place to prepare for the struggle outside. The pigs brought the struggle inside. They fostered race riots—vendettas between Black, Brown and White that lasted many seasons and cost many lives and lots of "added time." The prison became a fortress instead of a facility, a concentration camp instead of a Rehabilitation Center, a place unsafe for anyone who came off the streets who was knowingly involved in the struggle and anyone of us suspected to engage in the struggle upon release. We now consider ourselves as being "trapped behind enemy lines."

The pigs began their "inquisitions" by asking us intimidating questions in the counselor's office, at the disciplinary "kangaroo" courts and at the parole board hearings. Are you a muslim? A Black Panther? What do you think of . . .?, speaking of whatever group or individual that was controversial at the time. Your answers, your appearance and their suspicion determined your destiny. When this intimidation failed to stifle our resistance, they began a campaign of slow but deliberate "terror by murder"—assassinations followed one after another. "The list" went out to all the pens. It is the escalation of the nation wide attempt to "destroy the Malcolm X type prisoner," as Sister Kathleen Cleaver pointed out more than 2 years ago. In each case the pigs used another prisoner or group of Prisoners to play a Key Role in these assassinations in order to cover for themselves. In fact, it was carried out with such finesse that most of the prisoners refused to believe anyone could be responsible for this but another prisoner. It all came to light on January 13, 1970, when Doug Nolan, Cleve Evans and Alvin "lil Jug" Miller were assassinated on the "O-Wing" yard at Soledad Prison. This was the turning point, and retribution is without boundaries for these "three brothers of the spear."

Everyone's consciousness was raised to a higher level of understanding. It became suddenly evident that what the pigs had been conditioning us for all these years had begun. The symptoms and events leading up to this were the midnight raids where the pigs would come to our cells four and five deep, shine the light in our faces, wake us up, handcuff us and take us to "the hole" on either that same night, or a day or so later, drive us to another concentration camp without giving reason and without telling us where we were going. And we began to remember the brothers who all of a sudden got sick and went to the hospital but didn't return; and the stories about their deaths always came as a surprise because they were healthy the day before. The shock treatments and fright drugs they've been administering by force proves that there is more than one way to kill a man, that you don't always have to shoot him when enough torture and drugs and stress on the brain will kill the man or leave the body just functional enough to be put to work. And the fact that the pigs have always unleashed racist prisoners on our people in captive detention to rob, stab and kill only gave way to our development of a strong resistance movement that began to make it possible for Blacks to Survive. That has been our whole struggle in this world for 400 years and it is no less a struggle in order to survive for those of us caught behind enemy lines where the perpetrators of horror and death are waging a slow but deliberate campaign of genocide against us with the use of guns, drugs, gasses and poison, while playing it above suspicion.

Ours is the same cause as people everywhere else who find themselves the victims of man's inhumanity to man. And because we happen to be in America, where the forces of reaction and counterrevolution control the mass media and interpret events to their own advantage, does not isolate us from the liberation fronts of the Third World; and because we are imprisoned does not separate. Yes, we are indeed the revolutionaries—and to answer the question "why did I decide to struggle for liberation?": For the same as all of us our struggle is compulsory! We are bound to the camps of our enemies (where their strength is strongest and their force shows itself naked), armed only with the basic longing of oppressed people all over the world. It is this longing for life and this desire for freedom alone that compels us to confront the enemy.

Soledad
7-25-70

Dear Mrs. Roberts,

As a child in Louisiana, I remember crying once at the age of seven for being insulted because of my color, my mother cuddle me in her arms, and said a man ain't suppose cry, and from that day to this I haven't cryed. I had become immune to American insults to my dignity, after years of inurement. As I write this letter I find myself fighting with all my will to hold back my tears—not tears of sorrow, not tears of joy, but tears of a man who wants to fight for freedom & can't. I guess you could say my tears are tears of despair, wanting to fight for freedom and can't is the worst pain I have ever known. I hate America with a hatred that must be inconceivable to you for you have not known what it is to live with enforced inferiority haunting every step of your life from cradle to grave. I am honored that you were able to take time to write if I never see you Mrs. Roberts face to face to tell you how proud I am that you are fighting for freedom, I want you to know for your courageous stand your name is inscribed upon the table of my memory.

All power to the people;
Very Truly Yours
Otis P. Tugwell

Soledad
Aug., 1970

Dear Mrs. Stender:

I received the two books you sent to me today, to say a simple thank you, is not enough. Yet I can't find words to express my elation. Funny as this may seem to you, Mrs. Stender this is the first time I have ever received a gift from anyone. The greatest feeling that Man can have, is to feel that he is a part of something, to be wanted and needed, something to create a equilibrium between him and his doubts, and here in America I have had plenty of doubts and wonders. I watched with the memory of an elephant my black father drown himself in cheap alcohol to immune himself against hate and fear of this society. Some times I would sit by his side as a child do anyone that is dear to him, I would ask why he drank that stuff, and he would say boy go away and leave me alone. I would leave with tears in my eyes, because I wanted to help him. I knew that he was in pain. A child always desires to help the one thats dear to them and I was no different. I wanted to see and help him find his happiness, but I couldn't and I sensed that he knew it. I was too young at the time to understand the grip that bind him. Now as I look back, I can see that fear and dishonesty of America and trapped and immobilized him in the sunlit prisons of the American dream. The American dream to oppressed people now is a grimy filter of light and the more conscious we become the greater the distance between the dream and reality become. The personal and group violence this society has used physically as well as mentally to hurl black people into an obscure void, off into No man land. With legend, myth, coercion, fear and plain out right murder, she has driven the black man into a corner where he has to fight to live. How long did America think that we as a group of people would walk around in sheepish docility? While she perpetrated cruel and hideous acts against us. No man or nation is free from their crime America and you are no exception to the rule. Your civilization was built off of rape, murder, mutilation and robbery. For what you are, a malignant tissue of lies, you have lynched, exploited and lied your way to success, and freedom loving people throughout the world will put a sword through your criminal inhumane arid heart.

Looking back over my life as I write you this letter, I am forced to assess, and I can see that bitter railing is not effected enough to open this trap. Revolution is the only solution. All Power to the People.

Otis P. Tugwell

Folsom
Oct. 30, 1970

Dear Mrs. Stender:

I received your letter dated October 26, 1970. I found the information it contained encouraging. I can only hope that these efforts will be fruitful not only for those of us already here but for those yet to come.

I understand more than you realize, that this system will not change over night, nor will it change because of a sense of humanity on the part of those who run it. I am sorry to say that I do not fully share your optimism in the courts, but since I distrust them, that is only natural. Mrs. Stender, our overwhelming concern in here is not just correcting the injustices of adjustment centers and disciplinary committees, but rather the destruction of a system that does not serve its avowed purpose. Whenever I think of these places, I must take note that they have through Foster homes and institutions had full control of my entire 25 yrs., and the only thing I have accomplished is to have been a drug addict and a thief who may not even be allowed to go out and perform those self-debasing acts again. When I speak of I, it is more than just me, the three who were killed [shot on January 13, 1970, at Soledad], we met long ago, in W. L. Nolen's case it was Fricot School For Boys 1955, of the three first charged, Paso Robles and Preston, of the present seven these who are of my age or peer group we have known each other through the different juveniles. Of the young blacks here now Whiteside, Pinell, Poole we are all graduates of Preston School For Boys 1961. The point I am trying to make is that the system has had innumerable opportunities to help us and many many more, but yet it did not, but even there now that I look at it, I am wrong, they have helped us, in a way that they will never fully understand. They helped create the Malcolms and closer yet the Bunchys [Alprentice "Bunchy" Carter, a Black Panther murdered at UCLA in 1969] and Eldridges, and to a degree this system created you. They have helped nurture the very vanguard that will eventually ignite a flame, that no capitalist fire service can ever hope to extinguish, perhaps wishful thinking but more like an overdue awakening to something that has corrupted us all.

I am not saying these things to seem fashionable, I have been in rebellion all my life, I just did not know against who, nor how, but it's so clear now, that even a blind man cannot miss. As for the elected officials, promises of an investigation are a source of limited hope, but the problems cannot present themselves on any visits announced or unannounced, they would have to exchange places with us, experience the alienation of family, the fear of appearing humanly concerned for others, and therefore appear weak, experience the humiliation of going before parole boards, knowing you are ready but knowing before hand that you haven't enough time according to their formula. Tell them to live a day in and day out with a peer group that detests you for no other reason than he has had no contact with you and has accepted as truth all the myths for which this country is founded on, add to this a constabulary whose sights are limited who also consciously and unconsciously believe in and practice strictly on color but more on the classical class lines that capitalistic America embraced so fervently during the period immediately following the collapse of reconstruction in the South. In essence, the policy of using a false sense of identity with the powers to be as an excuse to degrade those beneath you, even to the point of provoking situations so as to furnish a plausible excuse to display your power. I doubt if our elected officials can ever arrive at these just conclusions, they are committed by choice to uphold the very system that supports and in turn is supported by these conditions. I do not doubt that some changes will be forthcoming, mainly through the dedication of those like you who see life as a continuous struggle to be humane and just. We here, some silently, wish to convery our deepest thanks for your continuous efforts in our behalf, but I feel that I must warn you that if we survive, if we remain true to our new found convictions, the institutions and life style you and others place faith and value in may well be destroyed. Some of us as you may well know are faking and merely being opportunistic, but even those pose a threat because you can fake to a point of no return. I hope you do not cringe or take affront to my openness and unsolicited philosophy but it is seldom any of us can try and explain our true selves.

Thank You For Your Patience
Venceremos
Raymond Parks

Folsom
Oct. 14, 1970

Dear Comrade:
. . . I've had some degree of exposure, and feel equipped to evaluate on my own as to the chance of meaningful change within the present system. And it will never happen baby, there are too many bourgeois people jiving about coming to the aid of the poor, oppressed, proletariat people. I speak of the bourgeois politicians black and white who are actually Capitalist oppressors themselves. Revolution is the only realistic answer. The installation of a new structure of government providing equal distribution for all the people, SOCIALISM. . . .

However, we can fool ourselves and continue to play the game of "You can make it if you try" for another hundred years if we like. . . .

All Power to the People
Caesar Moore

Soledad
1-1-70

Dear Comrade Robert,
It got very deep last night here New Years Eve. Over the years guys use to holler and act absurd at 12:00 but last night it was deep, quiet. I feel a new consciousness, difference, and solidarity was created. It's always been my understanding and feeling that consciousness comes when more of us are willing to feel it.

Comrades are strong; its deep man. Cultural nationalists and other cats that talk a bunch of shit aren't struggling for the same thing we are, they can't be, they are still wrapped up in the riot stage, hung up on identity and shit like that. They know nothing and do nothing but talk a bunch of rhetoric, we don't relate to that. We relate to the party, the weathermen, Mao, Che, Fanon, Lenin & Marx.

Like I mentioned to you comrade, the system blinds cats, destroys their mind and body if they let them. Like George said in his book* these places are to destroy a cat, no one leaves here a good guy in the way the system thinks they are, this place builds a lot of hate, love, and revolutionary spirit into a guy. When the prison gates open the real dragons will fly out.

I guess everything is said except Power and Love to the People:

Sincerely,
Fleeta Drumgo

Comrade Mine:

A few minutes ago I heard over the news the tragic melodrama played out by a group of my revolutionary brothers at the courthouse in Marin County.† These were not ugly men, not bad men, not callous or insensitive men; they were tired men. Men exhausted with white America's cruelty, the shame of legal due process, the duality of justice which nods understandingly at white citizens and marches with iron boots on the neck of black and brown citizens; tired to a point of insanity with the awful Frankenstein of the Department of Corrections.

Multiply their sentiments by the thousands and it will not be difficult to understand what I meant in one of my letters when I stated "the monsters made in California's racist, oppressive and

---

* George Jackson, *Soledad Brother: The Prison Letters of George Jackson* (New York: Coward-McCann, Bantam Books, 1970).

† Jonathan P. Jackson's attempt to liberate three black prisoners at gunpoint from the San Raphael Courthouse, Marin County, August 7, 1970.

sadistic prisons will be loosed on you tomorrow." Tomorrow is NOW!

The brother Christmas has served eight years in this prison system, each one harder to swallow than the one before it. He saw his black brothers beaten, driven mad, murdered; the brother McLain was a living mystery having served in so many administratively promoted race riots and survived; he too knew many a fellow brother who died quietly for nothing! Feeling what blacks in this nation are increasingly growing to feel: "if they must die then let the world know what it endeavors so hard not to see."

If the courts will not give black Americans justice, then black Americans will give justice to the courts. What happen today in that courtroom was exclusively manufactured by every judge in the state of California, every racist prosecutor, every lying public defender, every dog who commits horror on the black and brown brother under the color of law, with the impunity of justice to back him up.

No man, whether he be a judge, lawyer, prosecutor or policeman is exempt from the law of cause and effect. What California witnessed today by these three tired brothers was not the ending of anything but the beginning of self sought justice, liberty and dignity.

The courts, with its myopic judges, are more to blame for what happened in that courtroom than anyone else individually. For it is the courts which allow the cruelty of the Department of Corrections to exist, the court which permits a nigger and Chicano hating Adult Authority to continue its existence, creating mountains and mountains of hate with each month it meets, the court's which say "no-knock, no warrant, no evidence, no trial by adversary system but empty ritual played out by a stupid or indifferent public defender." . . .

When the court's change the people's respect for the law too will change.

All power to the People! Love and courage to the vanguard!

Thomas K. Clark

March, 1970
San Quentin

Comrades:

There is beauty in these convicts; there very affectionate, they have much love in them, they have a imperative need of the kindness, sympathy, understanding, and conversation of a woman, they regard love as a desire to be loved, one loves to be loved in return. Prisoners find it hard to relate to women, I mean that like this, they don't want to seem too agressive toward them, these guys have spent time in prison and aren't used to women and they want to be loved. The majority of them don't have a girl, there wives and love ones have betrayed them.

I'm sure there are those out there that don't recognize the real enemy, there minds are locked, and they have racist attitudes. Don't give up on them, you can reach them through love and understanding talk to them about there interest and, tell them that we are living in a crisis situation. We have always been. We oppressed people we must rid ourselves of imaginary insults, and direct that attention and energy on the enemy.

In prison there are also tools and fools. As Comrade Huey * said while confined that there are those who have a deep feeling of agony that comes from deprivation. They dream of getting out and getting a car a wife and house and the things that can make it better, and that dream makes it even more agonizing. Let me say that these are the tools in prison, the one who rat on people and, the bootlickers, you find them working in the offices of the pigs the passive, racist, reactionaries, however it should be put.

There is always madness going on in prison, one finds himself engage in all kind of petty intrigue which is necessary for survival, it consumes a lot of time and energy. But it is necessary.

The things which happen in prison are beginning to get in the air, I beg you not to let more defenseless men to killed, or tortured, you the people can end this it's as important as urgent as

* Huey P. Newton.

it is to end the war in Vietnam as employment, discrimination and other major issues facing the people today.

What I want to say is profound, it's difficult like I said when I see to unfold that which is in me, the words from my heart get caught up in throat.

I learn something awhile back that I was trying to run down to you and that is Revolutionary love encompasses tenderness too, I have had the feeling that I have fail to unfold tenderness then on second thought, I feel that I have unfold too much tenderness, which I feel has been confused with lust and gratitude, this aspect bugs the hell out of me, because the person I feel isn't receiving any of which I am sending. She must know in every word I write what I am saying is women me and you, love and war to the fullest extent.

Nobody can control my feelings but myself, nobody decides for me when or where I should lavish my affection, and dig, let me deal with the feeling subject I think it's in order, And I think you should know, that feelings need not make sense, feelings are sense, feelings are the pure and highest form of Revolutionary Consciousness.

All Power to the People,
Fleeta Drumgo

PS I am transforming pain into wrath, rage!!!

Soledad
November 12, 1970

Dear Fay:

I received your communication with the mail tonight. And it found me smack in the middle of a political orientation class consisting of many hungry confined minds here at Soledad Prison.

In the world of White Racism I'm a Nigger. In a world of changing values I'm a Black Man seeking harmonious conditions under the sun. Yet in my own eyes I am a striving revolutionary

MAXIMUM SECURITY

working to help create the reality of Che's dream of a "Love
Generation" welded together in a United Peoples Republic in
America, as well, as United Peoples world on the planet.

There's nothing greater than to see a prisoner happen by
slumped over with the weight of defeatism stacked on his back
like a ton of bricks; and after being showered with the beatific
essence of the rapid growing third world new order, shake the
weight of defeatism from his shoulder stand his full height, stick
his chest out, take in a deep breath and shout "all power to the
people," and really mean it. There is a beauty in that thats comparable to none. But each time the pigs pass my cell and look in,
I'm reminded of the price I will eventually pay. Nevertheless,
Right On!

All Power To The People!
A Brother in Arms and Truth
Earl

San Quentin
November 10, 1970

ALL POWER TO THE PEOPLE

RIGHT-ON!!

Dear Comrade,

When these few lines reaches your hands, I hope it finds all
well on the western front! As for myself, I will just relate it to
you as it is and will let you be the judge. And gain better insight.

I was approached by one convict while on the yard and was
told to watch out for myself. When I asked why, he said a
Officer (who has been continuously and consistently been harass-
ing me) came up to him the very day I was moved to the fifth
floor and said to him, not to mess with me, because I was a
trouble maker and Revolutionary who believes nothing but total
combat anyway, how, or manner!! That they had their eyes on
me and are keeping close track of my associates and who I talk
to. That if said inmate wanted to do his time easier with privileges
it would be beneficial to all parties concerned if he would pass

the word around to not to listen to me, not to get involved with me, and to let him know if I plan anything which would harass and become an embarassment to the C-D-C. The convict immediately brought the whole conversation to my attention.

Look, there isn't anything you can do or that really want you to do about my present situation, because I'm more than aware of my adversaries opinion of me or all Black and Consciously Aware People. Rather I want you to file this letter just in case some how I do come up an "accidental victim" of any violence.

But I'm more than aware of my shortness of time, life and breath and for this reason I feel compelled to relate my feelings as much as possible to you. So let this be a Manifesto of my determination. I have committed myself to speak out against all injustices perpetuated by those lower echelon members of this Gestapo type racist, irregardless of personal harassment, brutality and/or death. Now is the time not only to stand up and be counted, not to just give moral support, but, to rather seize the time, stand up and fight, be involved not only morally but physically! A lot of us will die, just as I may, but to die for a cause you have accepted willingly, faithfully, and determinedly is a cause well worth dying for. There is to me, no better death to die then the death of fighting for your freedom! The day of fantasy is over, it's time to be realistic now. It's not kill me if you want to, bur rather kill me if you can punk.

There is only one way to completely stop the revolution, and that is by destroying the world!!! There will be and cannot be more intimidations, peace treaties, negotiations or put offs. It's Revolution now or Death!! There cannot be no two ways about it. It's one or the other. People refuse to be pacified, lied to or intimidated any longer. And if necessary we should be able and willing to fight to the bitter end. Every man, woman and child. Liberation by any means!! Revolution now, permanently! Not on the installment plan!! And irregardless of any personal confrontations on my life, I refuse to be intimidated. I committed my life my entity to the liberation of my oppressed people. If I should die in the process it will not stop others who are determined and who live and breathe for the people. I refuse to lay down and negotiate any kind of settlement with the enemy. Look, revolution is no picnic or a circus. It's pain, torture, bloody and deadly death. There can never and have never been a Bloodless Conventional Revolution. All wars and Revolutions of history was a Death Dealing Revolution. I could never accept one what wasn't. I want to see my enemy dead! I can have no pity for this mad, vicious, crazy, hyprocritical dog. *And I am a Stone Revolutionary.*

Comrade Fay, with these words ringing in your ears and heart I will close.

Your Brother & Comrade

Larry

ALL POWER TO THE PEOPLE
ALL POWER TO THE VANGUARD
AND "POW" TO THE PIGS.
    "RIGHT ON"

Folsom
2-6-71

Dear Comrade:

As revolutionaries we should be, *and must be,* able to and have the talent and ability to organize and give direction not only to our *own* cadres and organs but to organize and consolidate effective and good faith coalitions and coalition relationships. In a word—if I or the comrades here cannot undertake to organize a coalition of elements in the prison who *recognize* that we have a certain commonalty of interests and goals into a viable, reciprocal alliance; then we are neither prepared nor evolved enough in revolutionary development to even *begin* to organize and/or educate the masses. We are pitifully inadequate for the task of educating or recruiting any element of the so-called "hard-hat" or "silent-majority" population, or any Lumpen who possess the "hard-hat" mentality. The concept of a coalition having been presented by professed non-revolutionaries, it is unquestionably the duty/obligation of revolutionaries to weld such a concept and such a coalition into a reciprocal instrument of revolutionary advancement.

I have discussed the above concepts with a couple of the comrades and they feel a cautious optimism in the matter. It is only a matter of less than three or four years that many of *us* were solely nationalists with all the resultant parochial motivations and interests. Today we identify with and relate to world humanity and have matured into a world consciousness.

All Power to the People
Comrade Robert

Folsom
August 7, 1970

Comrade Mine:

The child is called RESISTANCE.

The birth of this child is reason for optimism, but even that must be guarded; the child is yet an infant and must undergo much growth before he becomes relevant to the aims and aspirations, goals and hopes of those who labored with the pain of pregnancy which gave him life. From birth to maturity is a long way to travel. Wishing the child to hurry up is of no more consequence than wishing a human child being born tomorrow to become an adult the following day. Nature and her processes of evolution, much of which remains a mystery to us, is not sympathetic to our impatience.

It is wise of the parents to neglect the wish of a speedy growth and concentrate that and all other energy on the proper education of the child. In him must be placed a higher purpose than that which was inherited by its parents, it must be taught a sensitivity greater in dimension than what was taught to those who now hope for him to right the wrongs created by his parent insensitivity; in short he must be much more courageous in his convictions, stronger in the defense of just principles, wiser in his ability to discern between the right and the conventional, and braver about standing up for these things than the parents now who raise him. This is not an easy task, nor is it one which can be accomplished quickly.

Take your time, Comrade, and your revolutionary child will not have to raise his child for the same reasons you now raise him.

All Power to the People
Thomas K. Clark

Prison Law Project

The Prison Law Project was formed in January, 1971, by a nucleus of lawyers and nonlawyers who had been active in the legal defense of the Soledad Brothers, three blacks accused of killing a prison guard. They had become concerned about the California prison system as a result of the lawyers' experiences interviewing inmates who were potential witnesses in that case, and as a result of the information about prison conditions received in letters from inmates.

The lawyers began to make inquiries on behalf of prisoners and took some on as clients; they investigated allegations of arbitrary and illegal behavior on the part of prison guards and officials. They corresponded with inmates, many of whom have not had mail for periods of years.

Lawyers at the Prison Law Project file class actions as well as suits on behalf of individual prisoners whose rights have been violated. They attempt to obtain medical care for those who need it, and contact families and friends in order to increase visiting and correspondence. Those who are not lawyers assist in these activities. Through articles, books, and speaking engagements members of the Prison Law Project inform the public about prison conditions. By legal action and public education, the Prison Law Project is working to ensure prisoners the exercise of such rights as they legally possess, including especially the right to be free from psychic or physical brutality, and, by prison reform, to end the cruel and unusual punishment which is the lot of so many in California prisons.

Howard J. Berman
Bari Cornet
Sharon Damron
Richard Doctoroff
Jeffry Gleen
Brian Glick
Kathy Greenberg
Eve Pell
Patricia Roberts
Richard Spiegleman
Fay Stender
Deirdre Stone
Elaine Wender
Erik Wright